P9-CMF-204

Memorable Addresses

BY

American Patriots

FROM COLLECTION BY

JOHN CLARK RIDPATH

Breathes there a man with soul so dead,
Who never to himself hath said,
This is my own, my native land?
—SIR WALTER SCOTT.

ELLIOTT-MADISON COMPANY
CHICAGO

THE JONES BROTHERS
PUBLISHING COMPANY
CINCINNATI

Eloquence comes like the outbreaking of a fountain from the earth.
—DANIEL WEBSTER.

———

In eloquence, the great triumphs of the art are when the orator is lifted above himself; when consciously he makes himself the mere tongue of the occasion and the hour, and says what can not but be said.
—RALPH WALDO EMERSON.

———

There is no power like that of oratory.
—HENRY CLAY.

Contents.

Introduction.

NE of the earliest discoveries of the historian in his researches is that oratory has always ranked as the most dominant power wielded by man. Eloquence has been the equal gift of the untutored savage and the polished academician. In every age and among all peoples the orator has had his day and sway.

Oratory is well defined as the "masterful art." It has marked and precipitated the great epochs of man's evolution and progress. It is the flame or the flower of climacteric issues. It reaches such loftiness of logic, such a robustness of reason, such wisdom of wit, such aptness of appeal, such might of magnetism, as illumines it with inspiration, and gilds it with genius.

Great occasions produce great orators. The history of the American people has been peculiarly rich in those commanding moral issues which have been the chief inspiration of the highest oratory. This great new nation, founded upon, and the outgrowth of, new and lofty ideals of human relations, has made America the theater of some of the most striking and significant scenes in the vast human drama. Here was to be solved the problem of self-government. Here were to be fought to a finish the issues between autocracy, oligarchy, and aristoc-

5

racy, on the one hand, and democracy on the other, between the conservatism and selfishness of ancient customs and the new ideals of modern progress. Here the curtain was to fall upon the ancient system of human slavery. Here was to be sounded the knell of military conquest and aggression. Here were to be established forever the principles of free speech, free education, free religion, and equal opportunity.

Fired by the lofty inspiration of the new ideals, and encouraged by the freedom of speech unknown in the previous history of the world, the pioneer American citizen very early learned to mount some convenient stump in his "clearing" in the virgin forest, and, calling his fellows about him, there the original "stump-speaker" poured forth with great enthusiasm and effulgence his pæans of praise and his philippics of protest. From the stump he soon progressed to the pulpit and platform, the judicial court and the legislative forum, carrying with him his rugged and unyielding convictions and his fervid and unrestrained eloquence.

The result is that in the literature and annals of no other people is to be found such a vast amount and richness of oratorical production as in the American archives. And no task could one approach with greater hesitation than an attempt to collate and present in brief space typical examples of the best work of American orators.

Wherefore it follows that this little volume is submitted with great diffidence. It has been difficult to determine a standard upon which to base so limited a selection. The fundamental purpose of the compilation however is to awaken and stimulate an interest in and a love for American history. It has seemed best, therefore, to make selections for their epochal and illustrative values, rather than from purely oratorical and intellectual standards.

We sit as it were and behold the tragic events in the Drama of the Republic. The stage is set, the actors appear, recite their stirring lines, and disappear. In vivid and realistic settings we witness the Struggle for Independence, the Birth of the Republic, the Development of the New Nation, the Bitterness of the Civil War, the Downfall of Human Slavery, a Reunited Nation, the Sunrise of New Ideals, the Marvel of Modern Development, the Entrance of a Great New World Power, the Dream of Peace and Progress.

It has been a great pleasure, an inspiration, to wander at will through the vast and variegated garden of American oratory, to touch hands as it were with the great statesmen and thinkers who have builded and left for us the benign heritage of our free institutions, to find in them the fellowship and kinship of brain and brawn, of profound conviction, of keen passion, of lofty idealism, of fervid patriotism. And so this little garland of flowers—a memento and souvenir all too meager and inadequate—is presented to the reader in the hope that it may induce and encourage him to take up and view for himself the vast and inspiring and thrilling panorama of American history.

Resistance to Oppression.

PATRICK HENRY.

[*Delivered before the Convention of Delegates, Richmond, Virginia, March 28, 1775. This noble outburst of fervid and impassioned eloquence, born of fearless patriotism, was one of the most popular and influential productions preceding the War for Independence.*]

NO MAN thinks more highly than I do of the patriotism, as well as abilities of the very worthy gentlemen who have just addressed the House. But different men often see the same subject in different lights. I shall speak forth my sentiments freely and without reserve.

It is natural to man to indulge in the illusions of hope. We are apt to shut our eyes against a painful truth and listen to the song of that siren, till she transforms us into beasts. Is this the part of wise men, engaged in a great and arduous struggle for liberty? Are we disposed to be of the number of those who, having eyes, see not, and having ears, hear not, the things which so nearly concern their temporal salvation? For my part, whatever anguish of spirit it may cost, I am willing to know the worst and provide for it.

I have but one lamp by which my feet are guided, and that is the lamp of experience. I know of no way of judging the future but by the past. And, judging by the past, I wish to know what there

8

has been in the conduct of the British ministry for the last ten years to justify those hopes with which gentlemen have been pleased to solace themselves and the House? Is it that insidious smile with which our petition has been lately received? Trust it not, it will prove a snare to your feet. Suffer not yourselves to be betrayed with a kiss. Ask yourselves how this gracious reception of our petition comports with those warlike preparations which cover our waters and darken our land. Are fleets and armies necessary to a work of love and reconciliation? Have we shown ourselves so unwilling to be reconciled that force must be called in to win back our love? Let us not deceive ourselves. These are the implements of war and subjugation— the last arguments to which kings resort. I ask, what means this martial array if its purpose be not to force us to submission? Can gentlemen assign any other possible motive for it? Has Great Britain any enemy in this quarter of the world to call for this accumulation of navies and armies? No, she has none. They are meant for us, they can be meant for no other. They are sent over to bind and rivet upon us those chains which the British ministry have been so long forging.

And what have we to oppose to them? Shall we try argument? We have been trying that for the last ten years. Have we anything new to offer on the subject? Nothing. We have held the subject up in every light of which it is capable; but it has been all in vain. Shall we resort to entreaty and humble supplication? What terms shall we find which have not been already exhausted? Let us not, I beseech you, deceive ourselves longer. We have done everything that could be done to avert the storm which is now coming on. We have petitioned; we have remonstrated; we have supplicated; we have prostrated ourselves before the Throne, and have implored its interposition to arrest the tyrannical hands of the ministry and Parliament. Our petitions have been slighted; our remonstrances have produced additional violence and insult; our supplications have been disregarded; and we have been spurned with contempt from the foot of the Throne. In vain, after these things, may we indulge the fond hope of peace and reconciliation. There is no longer room for hope. If we wish to be free—if we mean to preserve inviolate those inestimable privileges for which we have been so long contending—if we mean not basely to abandon the noble struggle in which we have been so long engaged, and which we have pledged ourselves never to abandon until the glorious object of our contest shall be obtained, we must fight! I repeat it, we must fight! An appeal to arms and to the God of Hosts is all that is left us!

They tell us that we are weak; unable to cope with so formidable an adversary. But when shall we be stronger? Will it be the next week, or the next year? Will it be when we are totally disarmed, and when a British guard shall be stationed in every house? Shall we gather strength by ir-

resolution and inaction? Shall we acquire the
means of effectual resistance by lying supinely on
our backs and hugging the delusive phantom of
hope, until our enemies shall have bound us hand
and foot? We are not weak, if we make a proper
use of the means which the God of nature hath
placed in our power. Three millions of people,
armed in the holy cause of liberty, and in such a
country as that which we possess, are invincible
by any force which our enemy can send against us.
Besides, we shall not fight our battles alone. There
is a just God who presides over the destinies of nations, and who will raise up friends to fight our
battles for us. The battle is not to the strong
alone; it is to the vigilant, the active, the brave.
Besides, we have no election. If we were base
enough to desire it, it is now too late to retire.
There is no retreat but in submission and slavery!
Our chains are forged; their clanking may be
heard on the plains of Boston! the war is inevitable; and let it come! I repeat it, let it come!

It is in vain to extenuate the matter. Gentlemen may cry Peace! Peace! but there is no peace.
The war is actually begun. The next gale that
sweeps from the North will bring to our ears the
clash of resounding arms. Our brethren are already
in the field; why stand we here idle? What is it
that gentlemen wish? Is life so dear, or peace
so sweet, as to be purchased at the price of chains
and slavery? Forbid it, Almighty God! I know
not what course others may take; but as for me,
Give me Liberty, or Give me Death!

Farewell Address.

George Washington.

[This Farewell Address of Washington justly ranks as one of the great American classics. It was delivered to the American people in 1797 upon the completion of his second term as President. His declination to accept a third term has become one of the unwritten canons of American law which no succeeding President has dared to attempt to violate. The Address contains so much of the wisdom of warning and prophecy that it has ever stood as a guide-book for American statesmanship. Owing to the limitations of the present volume only extracts can be presented here.]

A SOLICITUDE for your welfare, which can not end but with my life, and the apprehension of danger, natural to that solicitude, urge me, on an occasion like the present, to offer to your solemn contemplation, and to recommend to your frequent review, some sentiments which are the result of much reflection, of no inconsiderable observation, and which appear to me all-important to the permanency of your felicity as a people. These will be offered to you with the more freedom, as you can only see in them the disinterested warnings of a parting friend, who can possibly have no personal motives to bias his counsel.

The unity of government which constitutes you one people is also now dear to you. It is justly so; for it is a main pillar in the edifice of your real independence, the support of your tranquillity at home, your peace abroad, of your safety, of your prosperity, of that very liberty which you so highly prize. But as it is easy to foresee that from different causes and from different quarters much pains will be taken, many artifices employed, to weaken in your minds the conviction of this truth; as this is the point of your political fortress against which the batteries of internal and external enemies will be most constantly and actively—though often covertly and insidiously—directed, it is of infinite moment that you should properly estimate the immense value of your national union to your collective and individual happiness; that you should cherish a cordial, habitual, and immovable attachment to it; accustoming yourselves to think and speak of it as of the palladium of your political safety and prosperity, watching for its preservation with jealous anxiety; discountenancing whatever may suggest even a suspicion that it can in any event be abandoned; and indignantly frowning upon the first dawning of every attempt to alienate any portion of our country from the rest, or to enfeeble the sacred ties which now link together the various parts.

For this you have every inducement of sympathy and interest. Citizens, by birth or choice, of a common country, that country has a right to concentrate your affections. The name of American, which belongs to you in your national capacity, must always exalt the just pride of patriotism more than any appellation derived from local discriminations. With slight shades of difference, you have the same religion, manners, habits, and political principles. You have, in a common cause, fought and triumphed together; the independence and liberty you possess are the work of joint councils and joint efforts, of common dangers, sufferings, and successes.

But these considerations, however powerfully they address themselves to your sensibility, are greatly outweighed by those which apply more immediately to your interest. Here every portion of your country finds the most commanding motives for carefully guarding and preserving the union of the whole.

The North, in an unrestrained intercourse with the South, protected by the laws of a common government, finds in the productions of the latter great additional resources of maritime and commercial enterprise and precious materials of manufacturing industry. The South, in the same intercourse, benefiting by the agency of the North, sees its agriculture grow and its commerce expand. Turning partly into its own channels the seamen of the North, it finds its particular navigation invigorated; and while it contributes in different ways to nourish and increase the general mass of the national navigation, it looks forward to the protection of a maritime strength, to which itself is unequally adapted. The East, in like intercourse with the West, already finds, and in the progressive improvement of interior communications, by land and water, will more and more find, a valuable vent for the commodities which it brings from abroad or

manufactures at home. The West derives from the
East supplies requisite to its growth and comfort,
and, what is perhaps of still greater consequence,
it must of necessity owe the secure enjoyment of
indispensable outlets for its own productions to the
weight, influence, and the future maritime strength
of the Atlantic side of the Union, directed by an
indissoluble community of interests as one nation.
Any other tenure by which the West can hold this
essential advantage, whether derived from its own
separate strength or from an apostate and unnat-
ural connection with any foreign power, must be
intrinsically precarious.

While, then, every part of our country thus feels
an immediate and particular interest in union, all
the parts combined can not fail to find, in the united
mass of means and efforts, greater strength, greater
resource, proportionably greater security from external danger, a less frequent interruption of their
peace by foreign nations; and, what is of inestimable
value, they must derive from union an exemption
from those broils and wars between themselves which
so frequently afflict neighboring countries not tied
together by the same government, which their own
rivalships alone would be sufficient to produce, but
which opposite foreign alliances, attachments, and
intrigues, would stimulate and embitter. Hence,
likewise, they will avoid the necessity of those over-
grown military establishments which, under any
form of government, are inauspicious to liberty, and
which are to be regarded as particularly hostile to

republican liberty. In this sense it is that your union ought to be considered as a main prop of your liberty, and that the love of the one ought to endear to you the preservation of the other.

These considerations speak a persuasive language to every reflecting and virtuous mind, and exhibit the continuance of the Union as a primary object of patriotic desire. Is there a doubt whether a common government can embrace so large a sphere? Let experience solve it. To listen to mere speculation in such a case were criminal. We are authorized to hope that a proper organization of the whole, with the auxiliary agency of governments for the respective subdivisions, will afford a happy issue to the experiment. 'Tis well worth a fair and full experiment. With such powerful and obvious motives to union, affecting all parts of our country, while experience shall not have demonstrated its impracticability, there will always be reason to distrust the patriotism of those who, in any quarter, may endeavor to weaken its bands.

In contemplating the causes which may disturb our Union, it occurs as a matter of serious concern, that any ground should have been furnished for characterizing parties by geographical discriminations—Northern and Southern, Atlantic and Western—whence designing men may endeavor to excite a belief that there is a real difference of local interests and views. One of the expedients of party to acquire influence within particular districts is to misrepresent the opinions and aims of other districts.

You can not shield yourselves too much against the jealousies and heart-burnings which spring from these misrepresentations; they tend to render alien to each other those who ought to be bound together by fraternal affection.

To the efficacy and permanence of your Union, a government for the whole is indispensable. No alliance, however strict, between the parts can be an adequate substitute; they must inevitably experience the infractions and interruptions which alliances in all times have experienced. Sensible of this momentous truth, you have improved upon your first essay by the adoption of a Constitution of Government better calculated than your former one for an intimate union and for the efficacious management of your common concerns. This government, the offspring of our own choice, uninfluenced and unawed, adopted upon full investigation and mature deliberation, completely free in its principles, in the distribution of its powers, uniting security with energy, and containing within itself a provision for its own amendment, has a just claim to your confidence and your support. Respect for its authority, compliance with its laws, acquiescence in its measures, are duties enjoined by the fundamental maxims of true liberty. The basis of our political system is the right of the people to make and to alter the Constitution of Government. But the Constitution which at any time exists, until changed by an explicit and authentic act of the whole people, is sacred and obligatory upon all. The very idea of the power and the right of the people to establish government presupposes the duty of every individual to obey the established government.

All obstructions to the execution of the laws, all combinations and associations, under whatever plausible character, with the real design to direct, control, counteract, or awe the regular deliberation and action of the constituted authorities, are destructive of this fundamental principle and of fatal tendency. They serve to organize faction, to give it an artificial and extraordinary force, to put in the place of the delegated will of the nation the will of a party—often a small but artful and enterprising minority of the community; and, according to the alternate triumphs of different parties, to make the public administration the mirror of the ill-concerted and incongruous projects of faction, rather than the organ of consistent and wholesome plans, digested by common councils and modified by mutual interests.

However combinations or associations of the above description may now and then answer popular ends, they are likely, in the course of time and things, to become potent engines by which cunning, ambitious, and unprincipled men will be enabled to subvert the power of the people and to usurp for themselves the reins of government; destroying afterward the very engines which have lifted them to unjust dominion.

I have already intimated to you the danger of parties in the States, with particular reference to the founding of them on geographical discrimination. Let me now take a more comprehensive view, and warn you, in the most solemn manner, against the baneful effects of the spirit of party generally.

This spirit, unfortunately, is inseparable from our nature, having its root in the strongest passions of the human mind. It exists under different shapes in all governments, more or less stifled, controlled, or repressed. But in those of the popular form it is seen in its greatest rankness, and is truly their worst enemy.

The alternate domination of one faction over another, sharpened by the spirit of revenge, natural to party dissensions, which, in different ages and countries, has perpetuated the most horrid enormities, is itself a frightful despotism. But this leads at length to a more formal and permanent despotism. The disorders and miseries which result gradually incline the minds of men to seek security and repose in the absolute power of an individual; and, sooner or later, the chief of some prevailing faction, more able or more fortunate than his competitors, turns this disposition to the purposes of his own elevation on the ruins of public liberty.

Without looking forward to an extremity of this kind, (which, nevertheless, ought not to be entirely out of sight), the common and continual mischiefs of the spirit of party are sufficient to make it the interest and duty of a wise people to discourage and restrain it.

It serves always to distract the public councils and enfeeble the public administration. It agitates

the community with ill-founded jealousies and false
alarms; kindles the animosity of one part against
another; foments occasionally riot and insurrection.
It opens the door to foreign influence and corruption, which finds a facilitated access to the government itself through the channel of party passion.
Thus the policy and the will of one country are
subjected to the policy and will of another.

There is an opinion that parties, in free countries, are useful checks upon the administration of
the government, and serve to keep alive the spirit
of liberty. This, within certain limits, is probably
true; and, in governments of a monarchical cast,
patriotism may look with indulgence, if not with
favor, upon the spirit of party. But in those of
popular character, in governments purely elective,
it is a spirit not to be encouraged. From their
natural tendency, it is certain there will always be
enough of that spirit for every statutory purpose.
And, there being constant danger of excess, the
effort ought to be, by force of public opinion, to
mitigate and assuage it. A fire not to be quenched,
it demands a uniform vigilance to prevent its burst-
ing into a flame, lest, instead of warming, it should
consume.

Of all the dispositions and habits which lead to
political prosperity, religion and morality are indispensable supports. In vain would that man claim
the tribute of patriotism who should labor to subvert these great pillars of human happiness, these
firmest props of the destinies of men and citizens.
The mere politician, equally with the pious man,

ought to respect and cherish them. A volume could not trace all their connection with private and public felicity. Let it simply be asked, where is the security for property, for reputation, for life, if the sense of religious obligation desert the oaths which are the instruments of investigation in courts of justice? And let us with caution indulge the supposition that morality can be maintained without religion. Whatever may be conceded to the influence of refined education on minds of peculiar structure, reason and experience both forbid us to expect that natural morality can prevail in exclusion of religious principles.

It is substantially true that virtue or morality is a necessary spring of popular government. The rule, indeed, extends with more or less force to every species of free government. Who that is a sincere friend to it can look with indifference upon attempts to shake the foundation of the fabric?

Promote, then, as an object of primary importance, institutions for the general diffusion of knowledge. In proportion as the structure of a government gives force to public opinion, it is essential that public opinion should be enlightened.

As a very important source of strength and security, cherish public credit. One method of preserving it is to use it as sparingly as possible; avoiding occasions of expense by cultivating peace, but remembering also that timely disbursements to prepare for danger frequently prevent much greater disbursements to repel it; avoiding likewise the accumulation of debt, not only by shunning occasions of expense, but by vigorous exertions in time of peace to discharge the debts which unavoidable wars may have occasioned, not ungenerously throwing upon posterity the burden which we ourselves ought to bear.

The execution of these maxims belongs to your representatives; but it is necessary that public opinion should co-operate. To facilitate to them the performance of their duty, it is essential that you should practically bear in mind that towards the payment of debts there must be revenue; that to have revenue there must be taxes; that no taxes can be devised which are not more or less inconvenient and unpleasant; that the intrinsic embarrassment, inseparable from the selection of the proper objects—which is always the choice of difficulties —ought to be a decisive motive for a candid construction of the conduct of the Government in making it, and for a spirit of acquiescence in the measures for obtaining revenue which the public exigencies may at any time dictate.

Observe good faith and justice towards all nations; cultivate peace and harmony with all; religion and morality enjoin this conduct; and can it be that good policy does not equally enjoin it? It will be worthy of a free, enlightened, and, at no distant period, a great nation to give to mankind the magnanimous and too novel example of a people always guided by an exalted justice and benevolence. Who can doubt, in the course of time and things, that fruits of such a plan would richly repay any temporary advantages that might be lost by a steady adherence to it? Can it be that Providence has not connected the permanent felicity of a nation with its virtue? The experiment, at least, is recommended by every sentiment which ennobles human nature. Alas! is it rendered impossible by its vices?

The great rule of conduct for us in regard to foreign nations is, in extending our commercial relations, to have with them as little political connection as possible. So far as we have already formed engagements let them be fulfilled with perfect good faith. Here let us stop.

Harmony and a liberal intercourse with all nations are recommended by policy, humanity, and interest. But even our commercial policy should hold an equal and impartial hand; neither seeking nor granting exclusive favors or preferences; consulting the natural course of things; diffusing and diversifying, by gentle means, the streams of commerce, but forcing nothing; establishing, with powers so disposed, in order to give trade a stable course, to define the rights of our merchants, and to enable the government to support them, conventional rules of intercourse, the best that present circumstances and mutual opinion will permit, but temporary, and liable to be, from time to time, abandoned or varied, as experience and circumstances shall dictate; constantly keeping in view that it is folly in one nation to look for disinterested favors from another; that it must pay with a portion of its independence for whatever it may accept under that character that, by such acceptance, it may place itself in the condition of having given equivalents for nominal favors, and yet of being reproached with ingratitude for not giving more. There can be no greater error than to expect or calculate upon real favors from nation to nation. It is an illusion which experience must cure, which a just pride ought to discard.

In offering to you, my countrymen, these counsels of an old and affectionate friend, I dare not hope they will make the strong and lasting impression I could wish—that they will control the usual current of the passions, or prevent our nation from running the course which has hitherto marked the destiny of nations. But if I may even flatter myself that they may be productive of some partial benefit, some occasional good—that they may now and then recur to moderate the fury of party spirit; to warn against the mischiefs of foreign intrigues; to guard against the impostures of pretended patriotism—this hope will be a full recompense for the solicitude for your welfare by which they have been dictated.

How far, in the discharge of my official duties, I have been guided by the principles which have been delineated, the public records and other evidence of my conduct must witness to you and to the world. To myself, the assurance of my own conscience is that I have at least believed myself to be guided by them.

Though, in reviewing the incidents of my administration, I am unconscious of intentional error, I am, nevertheless, too sensible of my defects not to think it probable that I may have committed many errors. Whatever they may be, I fervently beseech the Almighty to avert or mitigate the evils to which they may tend. I shall also carry with me the hope that my country will never cease to view them with indulgence, and that, after forty-five years of my life dedicated to its service with an upright zeal, the faults of incompetent abilities will be consigned to oblivion, as myself must soon be to the mansions of rest.

Relying on its kindness in this, as in other things, and actuated by that fervent love toward it, which is so natural to a man who views in it the native soil of himself and his progenitors for several generations, I anticipate with pleasing expectations that retreat in which I promise myself to realize, without alloy, the sweet enjoyment of partaking, in the midst of my fellow-citizens, the benign influence of good laws under a free government—that ever favorite object of my heart, and the happy reward, as I trust, of our mutual cares, labors, and dangers.

Funeral Oration for Washington.

HENRY ("LIGHT-HORSE HARRY") LEE.

[*Delivered at the Request of the Congress of the United States at Philadelphia, on December 26, 1799.*]

HE founder of our Federate Republic —our bulwark in war, our guide in peace, is no more! Oh, that this were but questionable! Hope, the comforter of the wretched, would pour into our agonizing hearts its balmy dew. But, alas; there is no hope for us; our Washington is removed forever! An end did I say?—his fame survives! bounded only by the limits of the earth, and by the extent of the human mind. He survives in our hearts, in the growing knowledge of our children, in the affection of the good throughout the world. And, when our monuments shall have been done away, when nations now existing shall be no more, when even our young and far-spreading empire shall have perished, still will our Washington's glory unfaded shine, and die not, until love of virtue cease on earth, or earth itself sink into chaos.

How, my fellow-citizens, shall I single to your grateful hearts his pre-eminent worth? Where shall I begin in opening to your view a character throughout sublime? Shall I speak of his warlike achievements, all springing from obedience to his country's will—all directed to his country's good?

Moving in his own orbit, he imparted heat and light to his most distant satellites. And, combining the physical and moral force of all within his sphere, with irresistible weight he took his course, commiserating folly, disdaining vice, dismaying treason, and invigorating despondency, until the auspicious hour arrived, when, united with the intrepid forces of a potent and magnanimous ally, he brought to submission the since conqueror of India; thus finishing his long career of military glory with a lustre corresponding to his great name, and in this, his last act of war, affixing the seal of fate to our nation's birth.

To the horrid din of battle, sweet peace succeeded; and our virtuous chief, mindful only of the common good in a moment of tempting personal aggrandizement, hushed the discontents of growing sedition, and, surrendering his power into the hands from which he had received it, converted his sword into a plowshare, teaching an admiring world that to be truly great you must be truly good.

Were I to stop here, the picture would be incomplete and the task imposed unfinished. Great as was our Washington in war, and as much as did that greatness contribute to produce the American Republic, it is not in war alone his preeminence stands conspicuous. His various talents, combining all the capacities of a statesman with those of a soldier, fitted him alike to guide the councils and the armies of our nation. Scarcely had he rested from his martial toils while his invaluable parental advice was still sounding in our ears, when he, who had been our shield and our sword, was called forth to act a less splendid, but more important part.

Possessing a clear and penetrating mind, a strong and sound judgment, calmness and temper for deliberation, with invincible firmness and perseverance in resolutions maturely formed; drawing information from all; acting from himself, with incorruptible integrity and unvarying patriotism, his own superiority and the public confidence alike marked him as the man designed by heaven to lead in the great political as well as military events which have distinguished the era of his life.

The finger of an overruling Providence, pointing at Washington, was neither mistaken nor unobserved, when, to realize the vast hopes to which our Revolution had given birth, a change of political system became indispensable.

How novel, how grand the spectacle! Independent States, stretched over an immense territory, and known only by common difficulty, clinging to their union as the rock of their safety, deciding by frank comparison of their relative condition to rear on that rock, under the guidance of reason, a common government through whose commanding protection, liberty and order, with their long train of blessings, should be safe to themselves, and the sure inheritance of their posterity.

This arduous task devolved on citizens selected by the people, from knowledge of their wisdom and

confidence in their virtue. In this august assembly
of sages and of patriots, Washington, of course,
was found; and, as if acknowledged to be most
wise where all were wise, with one voice he was
declared their chief. How well he merited their
rare distinction, how faithful were the labors of
himself and his compatriots, the work of their
hands, and our union, strength, and prosperity, the
fruits of that work, best attest.

But to have essentially aided in presenting to
his country this consummation of her hopes, neither
satisfied the claims of his fellow-citizens on his
talents, nor those duties which the possession of
those talents imposed. Heaven had not infused into
his mind such an uncommon share of its ethereal
spirit to remain unemployed; nor bestowed on him
his genius unaccompanied with the corresponding
duty of devoting it to the common good. To have
framed a Constitution was showing only, without
realizing, the general happiness. This great work
remained to be done; and America, steadfast in her
preference, with one voice summoned her beloved
Washington, unpracticed as he was in the duties
of civil administration, to execute this last act in
the completion of the national felicity. Obedient
to her call, he assumed the high office with that
self-distrust peculiar to his innate modesty, the constant attendant of pre-eminent virtue. What was
the burst of joy through our anxious land, on this
exhilarating event, is known to us all. The aged,
the young, the brave, the fair, rivaled each other

in demonstration of their gratitude. And this high-wrought, delightful scene was heightened in its effect by the singular contest between the zeal of the bestowers and the avoidance of the receiver of the honors bestowed. Commencing his administration, what heart is not charmed with the recollection of the pure and wise principles announced by himself as the basis of his political life! He best understood the indissoluble union between virtue and happiness, between duty and advantage, between the genuine maxims of an honest and magnanimous policy and the solid rewards of public prosperity and individual felicity; watching, with an equal and comprehensive eye, over this great assemblage of communities and interests, he laid the foundations of our national policy in the unerring, immutable principles of morality based on religion, exemplifying the pre-eminence of a free government, by all the attributes which win the affections of its citizens, or command the respect of the world.

Leading through the complicated difficulties produced by previous obligations and conflicting interests, seconded by succeeding houses of Congress, enlightened and patriotic, he surmounted all original obstruction, and brightened the path of our national felicity.

The presidential term expiring, his solicitude to exchange exaltation for humility returned with a force increased with increase of age; and he had prepared his Farewell Address to his countrymen,

proclaiming his intention, when the united interposition of all around him, enforced by the eventful
prospects of the epoch, produced a further sacrifice
of inclination to duty. The election of President
followed, and Washington, by the unanimous vote
of the nation, was called to resume the Chief Mag-
istracy. What a wonderful fixture of confidence!
Which attracts most our admiration, a people so
correct, or a citizen combining an assemblage of
talents forbidding rivalry, and stifling even envy
itself? Such a nation ought to be happy, such a
chief must be forever revered.

Pursuing steadfastly his course, he held safe
the public happiness, preventing foreign war, and
quelling internal discord, till the revolving period
of a third election approached, when he executed
his interrupted but inextinguishable desire of returning to the humble walks of private life. The
promulgation of his fixed resolution stopped the
anxious wishes of an affectionate people from
adding a third unanimous testimonial of their
unabated confidence in the man so long enthroned
in their hearts. When before was affection like
this exhibited on earth? Turn over the records
of ancient Greece; review the annals of mighty
Rome; examine the volumes of modern Europe;
you search in vain. America and her Washington
only afford the dignified exemplification.

The illustrious personage, called by the national
voice in succession to the arduous office of guiding
a free people, had new difficulties to encounter.

The amicable effort of settling our difficulties with France, begun by Washington, and pursued by his successor in virtue as in station, proving abortive, America took measures of self-defense. No sooner was the public mind aroused by a prospect of danger, than every eye was turned to the friend of all, though secluded from public view, and gray in public service. The virtuous veteran, following his plow, received the unexpected summons with mingled emotions of indignation at the unmerited ill treatment of his country, and of a determination once more to risk his all in her defense. The annunciation of these feelings, in his affecting letter to the President, accepting the command of the army, concludes his official conduct.

First in war, first in peace, and first in the hearts of his countrymen, he was second to none in the humble and endearing scenes of private life. Pious, just, humane, temperate, and sincere; uniform, dignified, and commanding, his example was as edifying to all around him as were the effects of that example lasting.

To his equals he was condescending; to his inferiors kind, and to the dear object of his affections exemplarily tender. Correct throughout, vice shuddered in his presence and virtue always felt his fostering hand; the purity of his private character gave effulgence to his public virtues.

His last scene comported with the whole tenor of his life; although in extreme pain, not a sigh, not a groan escaped him; and with undisturbed serenity he closed his well-spent life. Such was the man America has lost! Such was the man for whom our nation mourns!

Methinks I see his august image, and hear falling from his venerable lips these deep-sinking words:

"Cease, sons of America, lamenting our separation; go on, and confirm by your wisdom the fruits of our joint counsels, joint efforts, and common dangers. Reverence religion; diffuse knowledge throughout your land; patronize the arts and sciences; let liberty and order be inseparable companions; control party spirit, the bane of free government; observe good faith to, and cultivate peace with all nations; shut up every avenue to foreign influence; contract rather than extend national connection; rely on yourselves only; be American in thought and deed. Thus will you give immortality to that Union, which was the constant object of my terrestrial labors. Thus will you preserve undisturbed to the latest posterity the felicity of a people to me most dear: and thus will you supply (if my happiness is now aught to you) the only vacancy in the round of pure bliss high heaven bestows."

The Monroe Doctrine.

JAMES MONROE.

[From Message of President Monroe to Congress, December, 1823.]

N the wars of the European powers in matters relating to themselves, we have never taken any part, nor does it comport with our policy so to do. It is only when our rights are invaded, or seriously menaced, that we resent injuries, or make preparations for our defense. With the movements in this hemisphere, we are, of necessity, more immediately connected, and by causes which must be obvious to all enlightened and impartial observers. The political system of the allied powers is essentially different in this respect from that of America. This difference proceeds from that which exists in their respective governments; and to the defense of our own, which has been achieved by the loss of so much blood and treasure, and matured by the wisdom of their most enlightened citizens, and under which we have enjoyed unexampled felicity, this whole nation is devoted.

We owe it, therefore, to candor, and to the amicable relations existing between the United States and those European Powers, to declare that we should consider any attempt on their part to

extend their system to any portion of this hemisphere as dangerous to our peace and safety.

With the existing colonies or dependencies of
any European Power, we have not interfered, and
shall not interfere.   But with the governments
who have declared their independence and maintained it, and whose independence we have, on
great consideration and on just principles, acknowledged, we could not view any interposition
for the purpose of oppressing them or controlling
in any other manner their destiny by any European power, in any other light than as the
manifestation of an unfriendly disposition toward
the United States.

The True Grandeur of Nations.

CHARLES SUMNER.

[Extracts from Address Delivered in Boston, July 4, 1848. This Oration is justly regarded as one of the most chaste and lofty appeals to the noblest sentiments of mankind.]

IT becomes us, on this occasion, as patriots and citizens, to turn our thoughts inward, as the good man dedicates his birthday to the consideration of his character and the mode in which its vices may be corrected and its virtues strengthened. Avoiding, then, all exultation in the prosperity that has enriched our land, and in the extending influence of the blessings of freedom, let us consider what we can do to elevate our character, to add to the happiness of all, and to attain to that righteousness which exalteth a nation. In this spirit, I propose to inquire what, in our age, are the true objects of national ambition—what is truly national glory—national honor—what is the true grandeur of nations. I hope to rescue these terms, so powerful over the minds of men, from the mistaken objects to which they are applied, from deeds of war and the extension of empire, that henceforward they may be attached only to acts of justice and humanity.

In our age there can be no peace that is not honorable; there can be no war that is not dishonorable. The true honor of a nation is to be found only in deeds of justice and in the happiness of its people, all of which are inconsistent with war. In the clear eye of Christian judgment vain are its victories; infamous are its spoils. He is the true benefactor and alone worthy of honor who brings comfort where before was wretchedness; who dries the tear of sorrow; who pours oil into the wounds of the unfortunate; who feeds the hungry and clothes the naked; who unlooses the fetters of the slave; who does justice; who enlightens the ignorant; who enlivens and exalts, by his virtuous genius, in art, in literature, in science, the hours of life; who, by words or actions, inspires a love for God and for man. This is the Christian hero; this is the man of honor in a Christian land. He is no benefactor, nor deserving of honor, whatever may be his worldly renown, whose life is passed in acts of force; who renounces the great law of Christian brotherhood; whose vocation is blood; who triumphs in battle over his fellow-men.

Thus far mankind has worshiped in military glory an idol compared with which the colossal images of ancient Babylon or modern Hindoostan are but toys; and we, in this blessed day of light, in this blessed land of freedom, are among the idolaters. The heaven-descended injunction, "Know thyself," still speaks to an ignorant world from the distant letter of gold at Delphi; know thyself; know that the moral nature is the most noble part of man; transcending far that part which is the seat

of passion, strife, and war; nobler than the intellect itself. Suppose war to be decided by force,
where is the glory? No; true greatness consists in
imitating, as near as is possible for finite men, the
perfections of an Infinite Creator; above all, in cultivating those highest perfections, justice and love;
justice, which like that of St. Louis, swerves not
to the right hand or to the left; love, which like
that of William Penn, regards all mankind of kin.

The true greatness of nations is in those qualities which constitute the greatness of the individual. It is not to be found in extent of territory,
nor in vastness of population, nor in wealth; not in
fortifications, or armies or navies; not in the phos-
phorescent glare of fields of battle; not in Gol-
gothas, though covered by monuments that kiss the
clouds; for all these are the creatures and representatives of those qualities of our nature which are
unlike anything in God's nature.

Nor is the greatness of nations to be found in
triumphs of the intellect alone, in literature, learn-
ing, science, or art. The polished Greeks, the
world's masters in the delights of language, and in
range of thought, and the commanding Romans,
overawing the earth with their power, were little
more than splendid savages; and the age of Louis
XIV., of France, spanning so long a period of
ordinary worldly magnificence, thronged by mar-
shals bending under military laurels, enlivened by
the unsurpassed comedy of Moliere, dignified by the
tragic genius of Corneille, illumined by the splen-

dors of Bossuet, is degraded by immoralities that can not be mentioned without a blush, by a heartlessness in comparison with which the ice of Nova Zembla is warm, and by a succession of deeds of injustice not to be washed out by the tears of all the recording angels of heaven.

The true greatness of a nation can not be in triumphs of the intellect alone. Literature and art may widen the sphere of its influence; they may adorn it; but they are in their nature but accessories. The true grandeur of humanity is in moral elevation, sustained, enlightened, and decorated by the intellect of man. The truest tokens of this grandeur in a state are the diffusion of the greatest happiness among the greatest number, and the passionless Godlike justice, which controls the relations of the state to other states, and to all the people who are committed to its charge.

But war crushes with bloody heel all justice, all happiness, all that is Godlike in man. "It is," says the eloquent Robert Hall, "the temporary repeal of all the principles of virtue." True, it can not be disguised that there are passages in its dreary annals cheered by deeds of generosity and sacrifice. But the virtues which shed their charm over its horrors are all borrowed of peace; they are emanations of the spirit of love, which is so strong in the heart of man that it survives the rudest assaults. The flowers of gentleness, of kindliness, of fidelity, of humanity which flourish in unregarded luxuriance in the rich meadows of peace, receive un-

wonted admiration when we discern them in war,
like violets shedding their perfume on the perilous
edges of the precipice beyond the smiling borders
of civilization. God be praised for all the examples
of magnanimous virtue which he has vouchsafed
to mankind! God be praised that the Roman em-
peror, about to start on a distant expedition of
war, encompassed by squadrons of cavalry and by
golden eagles which moved in the winds, stooped
from his saddle to listen to the prayer of the humble
widow, demanding justice for the death of her son!
God be praised that Sydney, on the field of battle,
gave with dying hand the cup of cold water to the
dying soldier! That single act of self-forgetful
sacrifice has consecrated the fenny field of Zutphen,
far, oh! far beyond its battle; it has consecrated
thy name, gallant Sydney, beyond any feat of thy
sword, beyond any triumph of thy pen. But there
are hands outstretched elsewhere than on fields of
blood, for so little as a cup of cold water; the
world is full of opportunities for deeds of kindness.
Let me not be told, then, of the virtues of war.
Let not the acts of generosity and sacrifice, which
have triumphed on its fields, be invoked in its defense. In the words of Oriental imagery, the
poisonous tree, though watered by nectar, can produce only the fruit of death!

As we cast our eyes over the history of nations,
we discern with horror the succession of murderous
slaughters by which their progress has been marked.
As the hunter traces the wild beast, when pur-

sued to his lair, by the drops of blood on the earth,
so we follow man, faint, weary, staggering with
wounds, through the black forests of the past, which
he has reddened with his gore. Oh! let it not be
in the future ages as in those which we now con-
template. Let the grandeur of man be discerned in
the blessings which he has secured; in the good he
has accomplished; in the triumphs of benevolence
and justice; in the establishment of perpetual peace.

And peace has its own peculiar victories, in
comparison with which Marathon and Bannock-
burn and Bunker Hill, fields held sacred in the
history of human freedom, shall lose their lustre.
Our own Washington rises to a truly heavenly
stature—not when we follow him over the ice of
the Delaware to the capture of Trenton—not when
we behold him victorious over Cornwallis at York-
town; but when we regard him, in noble deference
to justice, refusing the kingly crown which a faithless soldiery proffered, and at a later day, upholding
the peaceful neutrality of the country, while he received unmoved the clamor of the people wickedly
crying for war. What glory of battle in England's
annals will not fade by the side of that great act
of justice, by which her legislature, at a cost of
one hundred million dollars, gave freedom to eight
hundred thousand slaves! And when the day shall
come (may these eyes be gladdened by its beams!),
that shall witness an act of greater justice still, the
peaceful emancipation of three millions of our
fellow-men, "guilty of a skin not colored as our

own," now held in gloomy bondage, under the Constitution of our country, then s ll there be a victory, in comparison with whi.. that of Bunker
Hill shall be as a farthing candle held up to the
sun.   That victory shall need no monument of
stone.   It shall be written on the grateful hearts
of uncounted multitudes, that shall proclaim it to
the latest generation.   It shall be one of the great
landmarks of civilization; nay, more, it shall be one
of the links in the golden chain by which humanity
shall connect itself with the throne of God.

As the cedars of Lebanon are higher than the
grass of the valley; as the heavens are higher than
the earth; as man is higher than the beasts of the
field; as the angels are higher than man; as he that
ruleth his spirit is higher than he that taketh a
city, so are the virtues and victories of peace higher
than the virtues and victories of war.

Far be from us, fellow-citizens, on this anniversary, the illusions of national freedom in which
we are too prone to indulge.   We have but half
done, when we have made ourselves free.   Let not
the scornful taunt be directed at us: "They wish
to be free; but know not how to be just."   Freedom
is not an end in itself; but a means only; a means
of securing justice and happiness, the real end and
aim of states, as of every human heart.   It becomes
us to inquire earnestly if there is not much to be
done by which these can be promoted.   If I have
succeeded in impressing on your minds the truths,
which I have upheld to-day, you will be ready to

join in efforts for the abolition of war, and of all preparations for war, as indispensable to the true grandeur of our country.

To this great work let me summon you. That future which filled the lofty visions of the sages and bards of Greece and Rome, which was foretold by the prophets and heralded by the evangelists, when man in happy isles, or in a new paradise, shall confess the loveliness of peace, may be secured by your care, if not for yourselves, at least for your children. Believe that you can do it, and you can do it. The true golden age is before you, not behind you. If a man has been driven once from Paradise, while an angel with a flaming sword forbade his return, there is another Paradise, even on earth, which he may form for himself, by the cultivation of the kindly virtues of life, where the confusion of tongues shall be dissolved in the union of hearts, where there shall be a perpetual jocund spring, and the sweet strains borne on the "odoriferous winds of gentle gales," more pleasant than the Vale of Tempe, richer than the Garden of the Hesperides, with no dragon to guard its golden fruit.

Let it not be said that the age does not demand this work. The mighty conquerors of the past, from their fiery sepulchres, demand it; the blood of millions unjustly shed in war crying from the ground demands it; the voices of all good men demand it; the conscience even of the soldier whispers "peace." There are considerations, springing from our situation and condition, which fervently invite us to take the lead in this great work. To this should bend the patriotic ardor of the land; the ambition of the statesman; the efforts of the scholar; the pervasive influence of the press; the mild persuasion of the sanctuary; the early teachings of the school. Here, in ampler ether and diviner air, are untried fields for exalted triumphs, more truly worthy the American name than any snatched from rivers of blood. War is known as the last reason of kings. Let it be no reason of our republic. Let us renounce and throw off forever the yoke of a tyranny more oppressive than any in the annals of the world. As those standing on the mountain tops first discern the coming beams of morning, let us, from the vantage ground of liberal institutions, first recognize the ascending sun of a new era! Lift high the gates, and let the King of glory in—the King of true glory—of peace. I catch the last words of music from the lips of innocence and beauty:

"And let the whole earth be filled with his glory!"

It is a beautiful picture in Grecian story, that there was at least one spot, the small island of Delos, dedicated to the gods, and kept at all times sacred from war, where the citizens of hostile countries met and united in a common worship. So let us dedicate our broad country! The temple of honor shall be surrounded by the temple of concord, so that the former can be entered only through the portals of the latter; the horn of abundance shall overflow at its gates; the angel of religion shall be the guide over its steps of flashing adamant; while within, justice, returned to the earth from her long exile in the skies, shall rear her serene and majestic front. And the future chiefs of the republic, destined to uphold the glories of a new era, unspotted by human blood, shall be the "first in peace, and the first in the hearts of their countrymen."

But while we seek these blissful glories for ourselves, let us strive to extend them to other lands. Let the bugles sound the truce of God to the whole world forever. Let the selfish boast of the Spartan woman become the grand chorus of mankind, that they have never seen the smoke of an enemy's camp. Let the iron belt of martial music which now encompasses the earth be exchanged for the golden cestus of peace, clothing all with celestial beauty. History dwells with fondness on the reverent homage that was bestowed by massacring soldiers on the spot occupied by the sepulchre of the Lord. Vain man! to restrain his regard to a few feet of sacred mold! The whole earth is the sepulchre of the Lord, nor can any righteous man profane any part thereof. Let us recognize this truth; and now, on this sabbath of our country lay a new stone in the grand temple of universal peace, whose dome shall be as lofty as the firmament of heaven, as comprehensive as the earth itself.

The Dangers from Slavery.

Theodore Parker.

[From a Sermon Preached in Music Hall, Boston, Sunday, July 2, 1854.]

HERE can be no national welfare without national Unity of Action. That cannot take place unless there is national Unity of Idea in fundamentals. Without this a nation is a "house divided against itself;" of course it cannot stand. It is what mechanics call a figure without equilibrium: the different parts thereof do not balance.

Now in the American State there are two distinct ideas—Freedom and Slavery.

The Idea of Freedom first got a national expression seventy-eight years ago. I put it in a philosophic form. There are five points to it.

1.—All men are endowed by their Creator with certain natural rights, amongst which is the right to life, liberty, and the pursuit of happiness.

2.—These rights are unalienable.

3.—In respect to these all men are equal.

4.—It is the function of government to secure these natural, unalienable, and equal rights to every man.

5.—Government derives all its divine right from its conformity with these ideas, all its human sanction from the consent of the governed.

46

That is the Idea of Freedom. It is derived from human nature; it rests on the immutable laws of God.

Next is the Idea of Slavery. Here it is. I put in also in a philosophical form. There are three points which I make.

First.—There are no natural, unalienable, and equal rights to life, liberty and the pursuit of happiness.

Second.—There is a great diversity of powers, and in virtue thereof the strong man may rule and oppress, enslave and ruin the weak, for his interest and against theirs.

Third.—There is no natural law of God to forbid the strong to oppress the weak, and enslave and ruin the weak.

That is the idea of Slavery. This Idea is founded in the selfishness of man; that is atheistic.

The question before the nation to-day is, Which shall prevail—the Idea and Fact of Freedom or the Idea and the Fact of Slavery; Freedom, exclusive and universal, or Slavery, exclusive and universal? The question is not merely, Shall the African be bond or free? but, Shall America be a Democracy or a Despotism? For nothing is so remorseless as an idea, and no logic is so strong as the historical development of a national idea by millions of men. A measure is nothing without its Principle. The idea which allows Slavery in South Carolina will establish it also in New England. The bondage of a black

man in Alexandria imperils every white woman's
daughter in Boston. You cannot escape the consequence of a first Principle more than you can
"take the leap of Niagara and stop when half-way
down." The Principle which recognizes Slavery
in the Constitution of the United States would
make all America a Despotism; while the principle
which made John Quincy Adams a free man would
extirpate Slavery from Louisiana and Texas. It
is plain America cannot long hold these two con-
tradictions in the national consciousness. Equilibrium must come.

So was it in the days of old: they ate, they
drank, they planted, they builded, they married,
they were given in marriage, until the day that
Noah entered into the ark, and the Flood came and
devoured them all!

Well, is this to be the end? Was it for this
the Pilgrims came over the sea? Does Forefathers' Rock assent to it? Was it for this that
the New England clergy prayed, and their prayers
became the law of the land for a hundred years?
Shall America become Asia Minor? New England Italy? Boston such as Athens—dead and
rotten? Yes! if we do not mend, and speedily
mend. Ten years more, and the liberty of America
is all gone. We shall fall—the laugh, the byword,
the proverb, the scorn, the mock of the nations,
who shall cry against us. Hell from beneath shall
be moved to meet us at our coming, and in
derision shall it welcome us—

"The Heir of all the ages, and the youngest born of time!"

To-day America is a debauched young man, of good blood, fortune and family, but the companion of gamesters and brawlers; reeking with wine, wasting his substance in riotous living; in the lap of harlots squandering the life which his mother gave him. Shall he return? Shall he perish? One day may determine.

Shall America thus die? I look to the past—Asia, Africa, Europe, and they answer, "Yes!" Where is the Hebrew Commonwealth; the Roman Republic; where is liberal Greece—Athens and many a far-famed Ionian town; where are the Commonwealths of Mediæval Italy; the Teutonic free cities—German, Dutch, or Swiss? They have all perished. Not one of them is left. Parian Statues of Liberty, sorely mutilated, still remain; but the Parian rock whence Liberty once hewed her sculptures out—it is all gone. Shall America thus perish? Greece and Italy both answer, "Yes!" I question the last fifty years of American history, and it says, "Yes." I look to the American pulpit, I ask the five million Sunday-school scholars, and they say, "Yes." I ask the Federal Court, the Democratic Party, and the Whig, and the answer is still the same.

But I close my eyes on the eleven past missteps we have taken for Slavery; on that sevenfold clandestine corruption; I forget the Whig party; I forget the present Administration; I forget the

Judges of the Courts; I remember the few noblest men that there are in society, Church and State; I remember the grave of my father, the lessons of my mother's life; I look to the Spirit of this Age —it is the nineteenth century, not the ninth; I look to the history of the Anglo-Saxons in America, and the history of Mankind; I remember the story and the song of Italian and German Patriots; I recall the dear words of those great-minded Greeks—Ionian, Dorian, Aetolian; I remember the Romans who spoke and sang and fought for truth and right; I recollect those old Hebrew Prophets, earth's nobler sons, Poets and Saints; I call to mind the greatest, noblest, purest soul that every blossomed in this dusty world— and I say, "No!" Truth shall triumph, Justice shall be law. And if America fail, though she is one-fortieth of God's family, and it is a great loss, there are other nations behind us; our Truth shall not perish, even if we go down.

But we shall not fail! I look into your eyes— young men and women, thousands of you, and men and women far enough from young! I look into the eyes of fifty thousand other men and women whom in the last eight months I have spoken to face to face, and they say, "No! America shall not fail!" I remember the women, who were never found faithless when a sacrifice was to be offered to great principles; I look up to my God, and I look into my own heart, and I say, We shall not fail! We shall not fail!

Plea for Slavery.

Alexander H. Stephens.

[From an Address on the Confederate Constitution, Savannah, Georgia, March 21, 1861.]

THE new Constitution has put at rest forever all the agitating questions relating to our peculiar institution. African slavery as it exists amongst us, the proper status of the negro in our form of civilization—this was the immediate cause of the late rupture and present revolution. Jefferson, in his forecast, had anticipated this as the "rock upon which the old Union would split." He was right. What was conjecture with him is now a realized fact. But whether he fully comprehended the great truth upon which that rock stood and stands may be doubted. The prevailing ideas entertained by him and most of the leading statesmen at the time of the formation of the old Constitution were that the enslavement of the African was in violation of the laws of nature; that it was wrong in principle, socially, morally, and politically. It was an evil they knew not well how to deal with; but the general opinion of the men of that day was that, somehow or other, in the order of Providence, the institution would be evanescent and pass away. This idea, though not incorporated in the Constitution, was the prevailing idea at that time. The Constitution, it is true, secured every essential guarantee to the institution while it should last, and hence no argument can be justly urged against the constitutional guarantees thus secured, because of the common sentiment of the day. Those ideas, however, were fundamentally wrong. They rested upon the assumption of the equality of races. This was an error. It was a sandy foundation, and the government built upon it fell when "the storm came and the wind blew."

Our new government is founded upon exactly the opposite idea; its foundations are laid, its corner-stone rests upon the great truth that the negro is not equal to the white man, that slavery—subordination to the superior race—is his natural and normal condition.

This, our new government is the first in the history of the world based upon this great physical, philosophical, and moral truth. This truth has been slow in the process of its development, like all other truths in the various departments of science. It has been so even amongst us. Many who hear me, perhaps, can recollect well that this truth was not generally admitted, even within their day.

The errors of the past generation still clung to many as late as twenty years ago. Those at the North who still cling to these errors, with a zeal above knowledge, we justly denominate fanatics. All fanaticism springs from an aberration of the mind, from a defect in reasoning. It is a species of insanity. One of the most striking char-

acteristics of insanity, in many instances, is form-
ing correct conclusions from fancied or erroneous
premises. So with the anti-slavery fanatics; their
conclusions are right, if their premises were. They
assume that the negro is equal, and hence con-
clude that he is entitled to equal rights and privileges with the white man. If their premises were
correct, their conclusions would be logical and
just; but, their premise being wrong, their whole
argument fails.

I recollect once hearing a gentleman from one
of the Northern States, of great power and ability,
announce in the House of Representatives, with
imposing effect, that we of the South would be
compelled ultimately to yield upon this subject of
slavery, that it was as impossible to war successfully against a principle in politics as it was
in physics or mechanics; that the principle would
ultimately prevail; that we, in maintaining slavery
as it exists with us, were warring against a principle, founded in nature, the principle of the
equality of men. The reply I made to him was
that upon his own grounds we should ultimately
succeed, and that he and his associates in this
crusade against our institution would ultimately
fail. The truth announced that it was as impossible
to war successfully against a principle in politics
as it was in physics and mechanics, I admitted;
but told him that it was he, and those acting with
him, who were warring against a principle. They
were attempting to make things equal which the
Creator had made unequal.

Gettysburg Address.

Abraham Lincoln.

[*Delivered at the Dedication of the Gettysburg National Cemetery, November 19, 1863.*]

 OURSCORE and seven years ago our fathers brought forth on this continent a new nation, conceived in liberty, and dedicated to the proposition that all men are created equal.

Now we are engaged in a great civil war, testing whether that nation, or any nation so conceived and so dedicated, can long endure. We are met on a great battlefield of that war. We have come to dedicate a portion of that field as a final resting-place for those who here gave their lives that that nation might live. It is altogether fitting and proper that we should do this.

But, in a large sense, we can not dedicate, we can not consecrate, we can not hallow, this ground. The brave men, living and dead, who struggled here have consecrated it far above our poor power to add or detract. The world will little note nor long remember what we say here, but it can never forget what they did here. It is for us, the living, rather, to be dedicated here to the unfinished work which they who fought here have thus far so nobly advanced. It is rather for us to be here dedicated to the great task remaining before us,—that from

these honored dead we take increased devotion to
that cause for which they gave the last full measure of devotion; that we here highly resolve that
these dead shall not have died in vain; that this
nation, under God, shall have a new birth of freedom; and that government of the people, by the
people, for the people, shall not perish from the
earth.

The New Day.

WILLIAM LLOYD GARRISON.

[Address at Charleston, South Carolina, April 14, 1865.]

 AM so unused to speaking in this place that I rise with feelings natural to a first appearance. You would scarce expect one of my age—and antecedents—to speak in public on this stage, or anywhere else, in the city of Charleston, South Carolina. And yet, why should I not speak here? Why should I not speak anywhere in my native land? Why should I not have spoken here twenty years ago, or forty, as freely as anyone? What crime had I committed against the laws of my country? I have loved liberty for myself, for all who are dear to me, for all who dwell on American soil, for all mankind. The head and front of my offending hath this extent, no more. Thirty years ago I put this sentiment into rhyme:

"I am an Abolitionist;
   I glory in the name;
Though now by Slavery's minions hissed,
   And covered o'er with shame.
It is a spell of light and power,
   The watchword of the free;
Who spurns it in the trial hour,
   A craven soul is he."

56

I said that in the city of Boston in 1835, and I was drawn through the streets of that city by violent hands, and committed to jail in order to preserve my life. In 1865, I say it, not only with immunity, but with the approbation of all loyal hearts in the city of Charleston. Yes, we are living in altered times. To me it is something like the transition from death to life—from the cerements of the grave to the robes of heaven. In 1829 I first hoisted in the city of Baltimore the flag of immediate, unconditional, uncompensated emancipation; and they threw me into their prison for preaching such gospel truth. My reward is, that in 1865 Maryland has adopted Garrisonian Abolitionism, and accepted a constitution indorsing every principle and idea that I have advocated in behalf of the oppressed slave.

But upon a broader, sublimer basis than that, the United States has at last rendered its verdict. The people, on the eighth of November last, recorded their purpose that slavery in our country should be forever abolished; and the Congress of the United States at its last session adopted, and nearly the requisite number of states have already voted in favor of an amendment to the Constitution of the country, making it forever unlawful for any man to hold property in man. I thank God in view of these great changes. Abolitionism, what is it? Liberty. What is Liberty? Abolitionism. What are they both? Politically, one is the Declaration of Independence; religiously, the other is the Golden Rule of our Savior.

I am here in Charleston, South Carolina. She is smitten to the dust. She has been brought down from her pride of place. The chalice was put to her lips, and she has drunk it to the dregs. I have never been her enemy, nor the enemy of the South, and in the desire to save her from this great retribution, I have demanded in the name of the living God that every fetter should be broken, and the oppressed set free. I have not come here with reference to any flag but that of freedom. If your Union does not symbolize universal emancipation, it brings no Union for me. If your Constitution does not guarantee freedom for all, it is not a Constitution I can ascribe to. If your flag is stained by the blood of your brother held in bondage, I repudiate it in the name of God. I came here to witness the unfurling of a flag under which every human being is to be recognized as entitled to his freedom. Therefore, with a clear conscience, without any compromise of principles, I accepted the invitation of the Government of the United States to be present and witness the ceremonies that have taken place to-day.

And now let me give the sentiment which has been, and ever will be, the governing passion of my soul: "Liberty for each, for all, and forever."

Vision of the Civil War.

ROBERT G. INGERSOLL.

[Delivered at the Soldiers' Reunion, Indianapolis, Ind., September 21, 1876.]
"Colonel Ingersoll speaks with a rare and enviable brilliancy."
—William E. Gladstone.

HE past rises before me like a dream. Again we are in the great struggle for national life. We hear the sounds of preparation—the music of boisterous drums—the silver notes of heroic bugles. We see thousands of assemblages, and hear the appeals of orators; we see the pale cheeks of women, and the flushed faces of men; and in those assemblages we see all the dead whose dust we have covered with flowers. We lose sight of them no more. We are with them when they enlist in the great army of freedom. We see them part with those they love. Some are walking for the last time in quiet woody places with the maidens they adore. We hear the whisperings and the sweet vows of eternal love as they lingeringly part forever. Others are bending over cradles kissing babes that are asleep. Some are receiving the blessings of old men. Some are parting with mothers who hold them and press them to their hearts again and again, and say nothing. Kisses and tears, tears and kisses—divine mingling of agony and love. And some are talking with wives, and endeavoring, with brave words, spoken in the old tones, to drive from their hearts the awful fear. We see them part. We see the wife standing in the door with the babe in her arms—standing in sunlight sobbing—at the turn of the road a hand waves—she answers by holding high in her loving arms the child. He is gone— and forever.

We see them all as they march proudly away under the flaunting flags, keeping time to the grand, wild music of war—marching down the streets of the great cities—through the towns and across the prairies—down to the fields of glory, to do and to die for the eternal right.

We go with them, one and all, we are by their side on all the gory fields—in all the hospitals of pain—on all the weary marches. We stand guard with them in the wild storm and under the quiet stars. We are with them in ravines running with blood—in the furrows of old fields. We are with them between contending hosts, unable to move, wild with thirst, the life ebbing slowly away among the withered leaves. We see them pierced with balls and torn with shells, in the trenches by forts, and in the whirlwind of the charge where men become iron, with nerves of steel. We are with them in the prisons of hatred and famine; but human speech can never tell what they endured.

We are at home when the news comes that they are dead. We see the maiden in the shadow of her first sorrow. We see the silvered head of the old man bowed with his last grief.

These heroes are dead. They died for liberty—they died for us. They are at rest. They sleep in the land they made free, under the flag they rendered stainless, under the solemn pines, the sad hemlocks, the tearful willows, and the embracing vines. They sleep beneath the shadows of the clouds, in the windowless palace of rest. Earth may run red with other wars—they are at peace. In the midst of battle, in the roar of conflict, they found the serenity of death. I have one sentiment for the soldiers living and dead: Cheers for the living; tears for the dead.

The New South.

HENRY W. GRADY.

[From Address at Banquet of New England Society,
New York, December 21, 1886.]

HERE was a South of slavery and secession—that South is dead. There is a South of union and freedom— that South, thank God, is living, breathing, growing every hour." These words, delivered from the immortal lips of Benjamin H. Hill, at Tammany Hall, in 1886, true then and truer now, I shall make my text to-night. Let me say that I appreciate the significance of being the first Southerner to speak at this board, which bears the substance, if it surpasses the semblance, of original New England hospitality— and honors the sentiment that in turn honors you, but in which my personality is lost, and the compliment to my people made plain.

My friends, we are told that the typical American is yet to come. Let me tell you that he has already come. Great types, like valuable plants, are slow to flower and fruit. But from the union of the colonists, Puritans and Cavaliers, from the straightening of their purposes and the crossing of their blood, slow perfecting through a century, came he who stands as the first typical American, the first who comprehended within himself all the strength and gentleness, all the majesty and grace

62

of this republic—Abraham Lincoln. He was the sum of Puritan and Cavalier for in his ardent nature were fused the virtues of both, and in the depths of his great soul the faults of both were lost. He was greater than Puritan, greater than Cavalier, in that he was American, and that in his honest form were first gathered the vast and thrilling forces of his ideal government—charging it with such tremendous meaning and so elevating it above human suffering that martyrdom, though infamously aimed, came as a fitting crown to a life consecrated from the cradle to human liberty. Let us, each cherishing the traditions and honoring his fathers, build with reverent hands to the type of this simple but sublime life, in which all types are honored, and in our common glory as Americans, there will be plenty and to spare for your forefathers and for mine.

Let me picture to you the footsore Confederate soldier, as, buttoning up in his faded gray jacket the parole which was to bear testimony to his children of his fidelity and faith, he turned his face southward from Appomattox in April, 1865. Think of him as, ragged, half-starved, heavy-hearted, enfeebled by want and wounds, having fought to exhaustion, he surrenders his gun, wrings the hands of his comrades in silence, and lifting his tear-stained and pallid face for the last time to the graves that dot old Virginia hills, pulls his gray cap over his brow and begins the slow and painful journey.

What does he find—let me ask you who went

to your homes eager to find in the welcome you
had justly earned, full payment for four years'
sacrifice—what does he find when, having followed
the battlestained cross against overwhelming odds,
dreading death not half so much as surrender, he
reaches the home he left so prosperous and beautiful? He finds his house in ruins, his farm
devastated, his slaves free, his stock killed, his
barns empty, his trade destroyed, his money worth-
less, his social system, feudal in its magnificence,
swept away; his people without law or legal
status; his comrades slain, and the burdens of
others heavy on his shoulders. Crushed by defeat,
his very traditions are gone. Without money,
credit, employment, material, or training; and
besides all this, confronted with the gravest problem that ever met human intelligence—the estab-
ishment of a status for the vast body of his
liberated slaves.

The soldier stepped from the trenches into the
furrow; horses that had charged Federal guns
marched before the plow, and fields that ran red
with human blood in April were green with the
harvest in June; women reared in luxury cut up
their dresses and made breeches for their husbands, and, with a patience and heroism that fit
women always as a garment, gave their hands to
work.

But what is the sum of our work? We have
found out that in the summing up the free negro
counts more than he did as a slave. We have
planted the schoolhouse on the hilltop and made it

free to white and black. We have sowed towns and cities in the place of theories, and put business above politics.

But what of the negro? Have we solved the problem he presents, or progressed in honor and equity toward solution? Let the record speak to the point No section shows a more prosperous laboring population than the negroes of the South, none in fuller sympathy with the employing and land-owning class. He shares our school fund, has the fullest protection of our laws and the friendship of our people. Self-interest, as well as honor, demand that he should have this. Our future, our very existence depend upon our working out this problem in full and exact justice. We understand that when Lincoln signed the emancipation proclamation, your victory was assured, for he then committed you to the cause of human liberty, against which the arms of man cannot prevail—while those of our statesmen who trusted to make slavery the cornerstone of the Confederacy doomed us to defeat as far as they could, committing us to a cause that reason could not defend or the sword maintain in sight of advancing civilization.

The relations of the Southern people with the negro are close and cordial. We remember with what fidelity for four years he guarded our defenseless women and children, whose husbands and fathers were fighting against his freedom. To his eternal credit be it said that whenever he struck a blow for his own liberty he fought in open battle, and when he at last raised his black and humble hands that the shackles might be struck off, those hands were innocent of wrong against his helpless charges, and worthy to be taken in loving grasp by every man who honors loyalty and devotion. Ruffians have maltreated him, rascals have misled him, philanthropists established a bank for him, but the South, with the North, protests against injustice to this simple and sincere people.

To liberty and enfranchisement is as far as law can carry the negro. The rest must be left to conscience and common sense. It must be left to those among whom his lot is cast, with whom he is indissolubly connected, and whose prosperity depends upon their possessing his intelligent sympathy and confidence. Faith has been kept with him, in spite of calumnious assertions to the contrary by those who assume to speak for us or by frank opponents. Faith will be kept with him in the future, if the South holds her reason and integrity.

The new South is enamored of her new work. Her soul is stirred with the breath of a new life. The light of a grander day is falling fair on her face. She is thrilling with the consciousness of growing power and prosperity. As she stands upright, full-statured and equal among the people of the earth, breathing the keen air and looking out upon the expanded horizon, she understands that her emancipation came because through the inscrutable wisdom of God her honest purpose was crossed, and her brave armies were beaten.

American Liberty.

HAMPTON L. CARSON.

[This gem of oratory and literature is taken from the Oration delivered by Professor Carson at the World's Fair, Chicago, July 14, 1893, on the Liberty Bell.]

THE institutions established by our fathers we hold in trust for all mankind. It was the Pilgrim of Massachusetts, the Dutchman of New York, the Quaker of Pennsylvania, the Swede of Delaware, the Catholic of Maryland, the Cavalier of Virginia, and the Edict-of-Nantes man of South Carolina, who united in building up the interests and in contributing to the greatness and the unexampled progress of this magnificent country. The blood of England, of Holland, and of France, wrung drop by drop by the agony of three frightful persecutions, was mingled by the hands of Providence in the alembic of America, to be distilled by the fierce fires of the Revolution into the most precious elixir of the ages. It is the glory of this era that we can stand here to-day and exclaim that we are not men of Massachusetts, nor men of Pennsylvania, nor men of Illinois, but that we are Americans in the broadest, the truest, and the best sense of that word; that we recognize no throne, no union of Church and State, no domination of class or creed.

American Liberty is composite in its character
and rich in its material. Its sources, like the
fountains of our Father of Waters, among the
hills, are to be sought among the everlasting truths
of mankind. All ages and all countries have contributed to the result. The American Revolution
forms but a single chapter in the volume of human
fate. From the pure fountains of Greece, before
choked with dead leaves from the fallen tree of
civilization; from the rude strength poured by
barbaric transfusion into the veins of dying Rome;
from the Institutes of Gaius and the Pandects of
Justinian; from the laws of Alfred and the
Magna Charta of King John; from the daring
prows of the Norsemen and the sons of Rollo the
Rover; from the precepts of Holy Writ and the
teaching of Him who was nailed to the cross on
Calvary; from the courage of a Genoese and the
liberality and religious fervor of a Spanish Queen;
from the enterprise of Portugal and the devoted
labors of the French Jesuits; from the scaffolds
of Russell and Sidney, and of Egmont and Horn;
from the blood of martyrs and the visions of
prophets; from the unexampled struggle of eighty
years of the Netherlands for liberty, as well as
from the revolution which dethroned a James;
from the tongue of Henry, the pen of Jefferson,
the sword of Washington, and the sagacity of
Franklin; from the discipline of Steuben, the
death of Pulaski and De Kalb, and the generous
alliance of the French; from the Constitution of

the United States; from the bloody sweat of France and the struggles of Germany, Poland, Hungary, and Italy for constitutional monarchy; from the arguments of Webster and the judgments of Marshall; from the throes of Civil War and the failure of secession; from the Emancipation Proclamation and the enfranchisement of a dusky race; from the lips of the living in all lands and in all forms of speech; from the bright examples and deathless memories of the dead—from all these, as from ten thousand living streams, the lordly current upon which floats our Ship of State, so richly freighted with the rights of men, broadens as it flows through the centuries, past tombs of kings, and graves of priests, and mounds of buried shackles, and the charred heaps of human auction blocks, and the gray stones of perished institutions, out into the boundless ocean of the Future. Upon the shores of that illimitable sea stands the Temple of Eternal Truth; not buried in the earth, made hollow by the sepulchres of her witnesses, but rising in the majesty of primeval granite, the dome supported by majestic pillars embedded in the graves of martyrs.

And thou, great bell! cast from the chains of liberators and the copper pennies of the children of our public schools, from sacred relics contributed by pious and patriotic hands, baptized by copious libations poured out upon the altar of a common country by grateful hearts, and consecrated by the prayer of the American people, take up the note of prophecy and of jubilee rung out by your older sister in 1776, and in your journey round the globe proclaim from mountain-top and valley, across winding river and expansive sea, those tones which shall make thrones topple and despots tremble in their sleep, until all peoples and all nationalities, from turbaned Turks and Slavic peasants to distant islanders and the children of the Sun, shall join in the swelling chorus, and the darkest regions of the earth shall be illumed by the heaven-born light of Civil and Religious Liberty!

The Blue and the Gray.

Henry Watterson.

[*Speech delivered at the National G. A. R. Encampment, at Louisville, Kentucky, September, 1895.*]

XCEPT that historic distinctions have been obliterated here, it might be mentioned that I appear before you as the representative alike of those who wore the blue and those who wore the gray in that great sectional combat, which, whatever else it did or did not, left no shadow upon American soldiership, no stain upon American manhood. But, in Kentucky, the war ended thirty years ago. Familiar intercommunication between those who fought in it upon opposing sides; marriage and giving in marriage; the rearing of a common progeny; the ministrations of private friendship; the all-subduing influence of home and church and school, of wife and child, have culminated in such a closely knit web of interest and affections that none of us cares to disentangle the threads that compose it, and few of us could do so if we would.

And the flag! God bless the flag! As the heart of McCallum More warmed to the tartan, do all hearts warm to the flag! Have you, upon your round of sight-seeing, missed it hereabout? Does it make itself on any hand conspicuous by its absence? Can you doubt the loyal sincerity of those who from house-top and roof-tree have thrown it to the breeze? Let some sacrilegious hand be raised to haul it down, and see how many gray beards who wore gray coats will rally to it! No, no, comrades; the people *en masse* do not deal in subterfuge; they do not stoop to conquer. They may be wrong; they may be perverse; but they never dissemble. These are honest flags, with honest hearts behind them. They are the symbols of a nationality as precious to us as to you. They fly at last as Webster would have had them fly, bearing no such mottoes as "What is all this worth?" or "Liberty first and union afterward," but blazing in letters of living light upon their ample folds, as they float over the sea and over the land, those words dear to every American heart, "Union and Liberty, now and forever, one and inseparable."

And why not? What is left for you and me to cavil about, far less to fight about? When Hamilton and Madison agreed in supporting a Constitution wholly acceptable to neither of them, they compromised some differences and they left some other differences open to double construction; and among these latter was the exact relation of the States to the General Government. The institution of African slavery, with its irreconcilable conditions, got between the North and the South, and— But I am not here to recite the history of the United States. You know what happened as well as I do, and we all know that there does not remain a shred of those old issues to divide us. There is not a Southern man to-day who would recall slavery if he could. There is not a Southern man to-day who would lightly brook the effort of a State to withdraw from the Union. Slavery is gone. Secession is dead. The Union, with its system of Statehood still intact, survives; and with a power and glory among men passing the dreams of the fathers of the Republic. You and I may fold our arms and go to sleep, leaving the younger men to hold and defend a property tenfold greater than that received by us, its ownership unclouded and its title-deeds recorded in heaven.

It is, therefore, with a kind of exultation that I fling open the gates of this gateway to the South! I bid you welcome in the name of the people, whose voice is the voice of God. You came, and we resisted you; you come, and we greet you; for times change and men change with them. You will find here scarcely a sign of the battle; not a reminiscence of its passions. Grim-visaged war has smoothed his wrinkled front, and whichever way you turn on either side, deepening as you advance—across the Chaplin Hills, where Jackson fell, to Stone's River, where Rosy fought —and on to Chattanooga and Chickamauga and over Missionary Ridge, and down by Resaca and Kennesaw, and Allatoona, where Corse "held the fort," as a second time you marched to the sea—

pausing awhile about Atlanta to look with wonder
on a scene risen as by the hand of enchantment—
thence returning by way of Franklin and Nash-
ville—you shall encounter, as you pass those
mouldering heaps, which remind you of your
valor and travail, only the magnanimous spirit of
dead heroes, with Grant and Sherman, and Thomas,
and McPherson, and Logan, looking down from
the happy stars as if repeating the words of the
Master: "Charity for all—malice toward none."

We, too, have our graves, we too had our
heroes! All, all are comrades now upon the other
side where you and I must shortly join them.
Blessed, thrice blessed, we who have lived to see
fulfilled the Psalmist's prophecy of peace:

"Peace in the quiet dales,
Made rankly fertile by the blood of men;
Peace in the woodland and the lonely glen,
Peace in the peopled vales.

"Peace in the crowded town;
Peace in a thousand fields of waving grain;
Peace in the highway and the flow'ry lane,
Peace o'er the wind-swept down.

"Peace on the whirring marts,
Peace where the scholar thinks, the hunter roams,
Peace, God of peace, peace, peace in all our homes,
And all our hearts!"

The "Cross of Gold."

William J. Bryan.

[*Address in National Democratic Convention, at Chicago, July, 1896. This splendid outburst of oratory won for Mr. Bryan, a comparatively unknown delegate, the first of three nominations for President of the United States.*]

I WOULD be presumptuous, indeed, to present myself against the distinguished gentlemen to whom you have listened if this were a mere measuring of abilities; but this is not a contest between persons. The humblest citizen in all the land, when clad in armor of a righteous cause, is stronger than all the hosts of error. I come to speak to you in defense of a cause as holy as the cause of liberty—the cause of humanity.

When this debate is concluded, a motion will be made to lay upon the table the resolution offered in commendation of the administration, and also the resolution offered in condemnation of the administration. We object to bringing this question down to the level of persons. The individual is but an atom; he is born, he acts, he dies; but principles are eternal; and this has been a contest over a principle.

Never before in the history of this nation has there been witnessed such a contest as that through which we have just passed. Never before in the

history of American politics has a great issue
been fought out as this issue has been, by the
voters of a great party. On the fourth of March,
1895, a few Democrats, most of them members of
Congress, issued an address to the Democrats of
the nation, asserting that the money question was
the paramount issue of the hour; declaring that a
majority of the Democratic party had the right
to control the action of the party on this paramount issue; and concluding with the request that
the believers in the free coinage of silver in the
Democratic party should organize, take charge of,
and control the policy of the Democratic party.
Three months later, at Memphis, an organization
was perfected, and the silver Democrats went forth
openly and courageously proclaiming their belief,
and declaring that, if successful, they would crystal-
lize into a platform the declaration which they
had made. Then began the conflict. With a zeal
approaching the zeal which inspired the crusaders
who followed Peter the Hermit, our silver Democrats went forth from victory unto victory until
they are now assembled, not to discuss, not to debate, but to enter up the judgment already
rendered by the plain people of this country. In
this contest brother has been arrayed against
brother, father against son. The warmest ties of
love, acquaintance, and association have been disregarded; old leaders have been cast aside when
they have refused to give expression to the sentiments of those whom they would lead, and new

leaders have sprung up to give direction to this cause of truth. Thus has the contest been waged, and we have assembled here under as binding and solemn instructions as were ever imposed upon representatives of the people.

We do not come as individuals. As individuals we might have been glad to compliment the gentleman from New York (Senator Hill), but we know that the people for whom we speak would never be willing to put him in a position where he could thwart the will of the Democratic party. I say it was not a question of persons; it was a question of principle, and it is not with gladness, my friends, that we find ourselves brought into conflict with those who are now arrayed on the other side.

The gentleman who preceded me (ex-Governor Russell), spoke of the State of Massachusetts; let me assure him that not one present in all this convention entertains the least hostility to the people of the State of Massachusetts, but we stand here representing people who are the equals, before the law of the greatest citizens in the State of Massachusetts. When you (turning to the gold delegates) come before us and tell us that we are about to disturb your business interests, we reply that you have disturbed our business interests by your course.

We say to you that you have made the definition of a business man too limited in its application. The man who is employed for wages is as

much a business man as his employer; the attorney
in a country town is as much a business man as
the corporation counsel in a great metropolis; the
merchant at the cross-roads store is as much a
business man as the merchant of New York; the
farmer who goes forth in the morning and toils
all day, who begins in spring and toils all sum-
mer, and who by the application of brain and
muscle to the natural resources of the country
creates wealth, is as much a business man as the
man who goes upon the Board of Trade and
bets upon the price of grain; the miners who go
down a thousand feet into the earth, or climb two
thousand feet upon the cliffs, and bring forth from
their hiding-places the precious metals to be
poured into the channels of trade are as much
business men as the few financial magnates who,
in a back room, corner the money of the world.
We come to speak of this broader class of business men.

Ah, my friends, we say not one word against
those who live upon the Atlantic Coast. But the
hardy pioneers who have braved all the dangers
of the wilderness, who have made the desert to
blossom as the rose—the pioneers away out there
(pointing to the West), who rear their children
near to Nature's heart, where they can mingle
their voices with the voices of the birds,—out
there where they have erected schoolhouses for the
education of their young, churches where they
praise their Creator, and cemeteries where rest

the ashes of their dead—these people, we say are as deserving of the consideration of our party as any people in this country. It is for these that we speak. We do not come as aggressors. Our war is not a war of conquest; we are fighting in the defense of our homes, our families, and posterity. We have petitioned, and our petitions have been scorned; we have entreated, and our entreaties have been disregarded; we have begged, and they have mocked when our calamity came. We beg no longer; we entreat no more; we petition no more. We defy them!

The gentleman from Wisconsin has said that he fears a Robespierre. My friends, in this land of the free you need not fear that a tyrant will spring up from among the people. What we need is an Andrew Jackson to stand, as Jackson stood, against the encroachments of organized wealth.

They tell us that this platform was made to catch votes. We reply to them that changing conditions make new issues; that the principles upon which democracy rests are as everlasting as the hills, but that they must be applied to new conditions as they arise. Conditions have arisen, and we are here to meet those conditions. They tell us that the income tax ought not to be brought in here; that it is a new idea. They criticize us for our criticism of the Supreme Court of the United States. My friends, we have not criticized; we have simply called attention to what you already know. If you want criticisms, read the dissenting opinions of the court. There you will find criticisms. They say that we passed an unconstitutional law; we deny it. The income tax law was not unconstitutional when it was passed; it was not unconstitutional when it went before the Supreme Court for the first time; it did not become unconstitutional until one of the judges changed his mind, and we can not be expected to know when a judge will change his mind. The income tax is just. It simply intends to put the burdens of government justly upon the backs of the people. I am in favor of an income tax. When I find a man who is not willing to bear his share of the burdens of the government which protects him, I find a man who is unworthy to enjoy the blessings of a government like ours.

They say that we are opposing national bank currency; it is true. If you will read what Thomas Benton said, you will find he said that, in searching history, he could find but one parallel to Andrew Jackson; that was Cicero, who destroyed the conspiracy of Cataline and saved Rome. Benton said that Cicero only did for Rome what Jackson did for us when he destroyed the bank conspiracy and saved America. We say in our platform that we believe that the right to coin and issue money is a function of government. We believe it. We believe that it is a part of sovereignty, and can no more with safety be delegated to private individuals than we could afford to delegate to private individuals the power to make penal statutes or levy taxes. Mr. Jefferson, who was once regarded as good Democratic authority, seems to have differed in opinion from the gentleman who has addressed us on the part of the minority. Those who are opposed to this proposition tell us that the issue of paper money is a function of the bank, and that the government ought to go out of the banking business. I stand with Jefferson rather than with them, and tell them, as he did, that the issue of money is a function of government, and that the banks ought to go out of the governing business.

They complain about the plank which declares against life tenure in office. They have tried to strain it to mean that which it does not mean. What we oppose by that plank is the life tenure which is being built up in Washington, and which excludes from participation in official benefits the humbler members of society.

Let me call your attention to two or three important things. The gentleman from New York says that he will propose an amendment to the platform, providing that the proposed change in our monetary system shall not affect contracts already made. Let me remind you that there is no intention of affecting those contracts, which, according to present laws, are made payable in gold; but if he means to say that we can not change our monetary system without protecting those who have loaned money before the change was made, I desire to ask him where, in law or

in morals, he can find justification for not protecting the debtors when the act of 1873 was
passed, if he now insists that we must protect the
creditors.

He says he will also propose an amendment
which will provide for the suspension of free
coinage if we fail to maintain the parity within a
year. We reply that when we advocate a policy
which we believe will be successful we are not
compelled to raise a doubt as to our own sincerity by suggesting what we shall do if we fail.
I ask him, if he would apply his logic to us, why
he does not apply it to himself. He says he
wants this country to try to secure an international agreement. Why does he not tell us what
he is going to do if he fails to secure an international agreement? There is more reason for him
to do that than there is for us to provide against
the failure to maintain the parity. Our opponents
have tried for twenty years to secure an international agreement, and those are waiting for it
most patiently who do not want it at all.

And now, my friends, let me come to the paramount issue. If they ask us why it is that we say
more on the money question than we say upon the
tariff question, I reply that, if protection has slain
its thousands, the gold standard has slain its tens
of thousands. If they ask us why we do not embody
in our platform all the things that we believe in,
we reply that when we have restored the money
of the Constitution all other necessary reforms will

be possible; but that until this is done there is no other reform that can be accomplished.

Why is it that within three months such a change has come over the country? Three months ago, when it was confidently asserted that those who believe in the gold standard would frame our platform and nominate our candidates, even the advocates of the gold standard did not think that we could elect a President. And they had good reason for their doubt, because there is scarcely a State here to-day asking for the gold standard which is not in absolute control of the Republican party. But note the change. Mr. McKinley was nominated at St. Louis upon a platform which declared for the maintenance of the gold standard until it can be changed into bimetallism by international agreement. Mr. McKinley was the most popular man among the Republicans, and three months ago everybody in the Republican party prophesied his election. How is it to-day? Why, the man who was once pleased to think that he looked like Napoleon—that man shudders to-day when he remembers that he was nominated on the anniversary of the battle of Waterloo. Not only that, but as he listens he can hear with ever-increasing distinctness the sound of the waves as they beat upon the lonely shores of St. Helena.

Why this change? Ah, my friends, is not the reason for the change evident to any one who will look at the matter? No private character, however pure, no personal popularity, however great, can

protect from the avenging wrath of an indignant
people a man who will declare that he is in favor
of fastening the gold standard upon this country,
or who is willing to surrender the right of self-
government and place the legislative control of
our affairs in the hands of foreign potentates and
powers.

We go forth confident that we shall win. Why?
Because upon the paramount issue of this campaign
there is not a spot of ground upon which the
enemy will dare to challenge battle. If they tell
us that the gold standard is a good thing, we
shall point to their platform and tell them that
their platform pledges the party to get rid of the
gold standard and substitute bimetallism. If the
gold standard is a good thing, why try to get rid
of it? I call your attention to the fact that some
of the very people who are in this convention
to-day and who tell us that we ought to declare in
favor of international bimetallism—thereby declaring that the gold standard is wrong and that the
principle of bimetallism is better—these very people
four months ago were open and avowed advocates of the gold standard, and were then telling
us that we could not legislate two metals together,
even with the aid of all the world. If the gold
standard is a good thing, we ought to declare in
favor of its retention and not in favor of aban-
doning it; and if the gold standard is a bad thing
why should we wait until other nations are willing
to help us to let go? Here is the line of battle,

and we care not upon which issue they force the fight; we are prepared to meet them on either issue or on both. If they tell us that the gold standard is the standard of civilization, we reply to them that this, the most enlightened of all the nations of the earth, has never declared for a gold standard, and that both the great parties this year are declaring against it. If the gold standard is the standard of civilization, why, my friends, should we not have it? If they come to meet us on that issue we can present the history of our nation. More than that; we can tell them that they will search the pages of history in vain to find a single instance where the common people of any land have ever declared themselves in favor of the gold standard. They can find where the holders of fixed investments have declared for a gold standard, but not where the masses have.

Mr. Carlisle said in 1878 that this was a struggle between "the idle holders of idle capital" and "the struggling masses who produce the wealth and pay the taxes of the country;" and, my friends, the question we are to decide is: Upon which side will the Democratic party fight; upon the side of the idle holders of idle capital", or upon the side of the "struggling masses"? That is the question which the party must answer first, and then it must be answered by each individual hereafter. The sympathies of the Democratic party, as shown by the platform, are on the side of the struggling masses who have ever been the foundation of the

Democratic party. There are two ideas of government. There are those who believe that, if you will only legislate to make the well-to-do prosperous, their prosperity will leak through on those below. The Democratic idea, however, has been that if you legislate to make the masses prosperous, their prosperity will find its way up through every class which rests upon them.

You come to us and tell us that the great cities are in favor of the gold standard; we reply that the great cities rest upon our broad and fertile prairies. Burn down your cities and leave our farms, and your cities will spring up again as if by magic; but destroy our farms and the grass will grow in the streets of every city in the country.

My friends, we declare that this nation is able to legislate for its own people on every question, without waiting for the aid or consent of any other nation on earth; and upon that issue we expect to carry every State in the Union. I shall not slander the inhabitants of the fair State of Massachusetts nor the inhabitants of the State of New York by saying that, when they are confronted with the proposition, they will declare that this nation is not able to attend to its own business. It is the issue of 1776 over again. Our ancestors, when but three millions in number, had the courage to declare their political independence of every other nation; shall we, their descendants, when we have grown to seventy millions, declare that we are less independent than our forefathers? No, my friends, that will never be the verdict of our people. Therefore, we care not upon what lines the battle is fought. If they say bimetallism is good but that we can not have it until other nations help us, we reply that, instead of having a gold standard because England has, we will restore bimetallism, and then let England have bimetallism because the United States has it. If they dare to come out in the open field and defend the gold standard as a good thing, we will fight them to the uttermost. Having behind us the producing masses of this nation and the world, supported by the commercial interests, the laboring interests, and the toilers everywhere, we will answer their demand for a gold standard by saying to them: You shall not press down upon the brow of labor this crown of thorns, you shall not crucify mankind upon a cross of gold.

International Amity.

William McKinley.

[*Address at Pan-American Exposition, Buffalo, N. Y., September 5, 1901.*]

"*So he delivered his now famous Buffalo speech. It was heard around the world. Throughout Christendom one expression caught the imagination of men—'God and man have linked the nations together. No nation can longer be indifferent to any other.' This gospel of commercial amity and of peaceful rivalry, this recognition of the Golden Rule in the relations of nations, coming from the lips of the former apostle of protection, naturally startled the many who did not know how rapidly and how splendidly his philosophy had broadened. It was no revelation to those who knew that his greatest pride was felt in the unification of his own people, and that now his fondest ambition was to apply the same principle to world relations, primarily for the good of America, ultimately for the good of all nations. It reads like a benediction.*"—Walter Wellman, in Review of Reviews.

 AM glad to be again in the city of Buffalo and exchange greetings with her people, to whose generous hospitality I am not a stranger, and with whose good-will I have been repeatedly and signally honored. To-day, I have additional satisfaction in meeting and giving welcome to the foreign representatives assembled here, whose presence and participation in this exposition have contributed in so marked a degree to its interest and success. To the commissioners of the Dominion of Canada and the British Colonies, the French Colonies, the Republics of Mexico and of Central and South America, and the commissioners of Cuba and Porto Rico, who share with us in this undertaking, we give the hand of fellowship and felicitate with them upon the triumphs of art, science, education, and manufacture which the old has bequeathed to the new century.

Expositions are the timekeepers of progress. They record the world's advancement. They stimulate the energy, enterprise, and intellect of the people, and quicken human genius. They go into the home. They broaden and brighten the daily life of the people. They open mighty storehouses of information to the student. Every exposition, great or small, has helped to some onward step. Comparison of ideas is always educational, and as such instructs the brain and hand of man. Friendly rivalry follows, which is the spur to industrial improvement, the inspiration to useful invention and to high endeavor in all departments of human activity. It exacts a study of the wants, comforts, and even the whims of the people, and recognizes the efficacy of high quality and new prices to win their favor. The quest for trade is an incentive to men of business to devise, invent, improve, and economize in the cost of production. Business life, whether among ourselves or with other people, is ever a sharp struggle for success. It will be none the less so in the future. Without competition we would be clinging to the clumsy and antiquated processes of farming and manufacture and the methods of business of long ago, and the twentieth would be no further advanced than the eighteenth century. But though commercial competitors we are, commercial enemies we must not be.

The Pan-American Exposition has done its work thoroughly, presenting in its exhibits evidences of the highest skill, and illustrating the progress of the human family in the western hemisphere. This portion of the earth has no cause for humiliation for the part it has performed in the march of civilization. It has not accomplished everything; far from it. It has simply done its best; and without vanity or boastfulness, and recognizing the manifold achievements of others, it invites the friendly rivalry of all the powers in the peaceful pursuits of trade and commerce, and will co-operate with all in advancing the highest and best interests of humanity. The wisdom and energy of all the nations are none too great for the world's work. The success of art, science, industry, and invention is an international asset, and a common glory.

After all, how near one to the other is every part of the world! Modern inventions have brought into close relation widely separated peoples and made them better acquainted. Geographic and political divisions will continue to exist, but distances have been effaced. Swift ships and fast trains are becoming cosmopolitan. They invade fields which a few years ago were impenetrable. The world's products are exchanged as never before, and with increasing knowledge and larger trade. Prices are fixed with mathematical precision by supply and demand. The world's selling prices are regulated by market and crop reports. We travel greater distances in shorter spaces of time and with more ease than was ever dreamed of by the fathers. Isolation is no longer possible or desirable. The same important news is read, though in different languages, the same day in all Christendom. The telegraph keeps us advised of what is occurring everywhere, and the press foreshadows, with more or less accuracy, the plans and purposes of the nations. Market prices of products and of securities are hourly known in every commercial mart, and the investments of the people extend beyond their own national boundaries into the remotest parts of the earth. Vast transactions are conducted, and the international exchanges are made, by the tick of the cable. Every event of interest is immediately bulletined. The quick gathering and transmission of news, like rapid transit, are of recent origin, and are only made possible by the genius of the inventor and the courage of the investor.

It took a special messenger of the Government, with every facility known at the time for rapid travel, nineteen days to go from the city of Washington to New Orleans with a message to General Jackson that the war with England had ceased and a treaty of peace had been signed. How different now! We reached General Miles in Porto Rico by cable, and he was able, through the military telegraph, to stop his army on the firing line with the message that the United States and Spain had signed a protocol suspending hostilities. We knew almost instantly of the first shots fired at Santiago,

and the subsequent surrender of the Spanish forces
was known at Washington within less than an hour
of its consummation. The first ship of Cervera's
fleet had hardly emerged from that historic harbor
when the fact was flashed to our capital, and the
swift destruction that followed was announced immediately through the wonderful medium of teleg-
raphy. So accustomed are we to safe and easy
communication with distant lands that its temporary
interruption, even in ordinary times, results in loss
and inconvenience. We shall never forget the
days of anxious waiting and awful suspense when
no informatiin was permitted to be sent from
Peking, and the diplomatic representatives of the
nations in China, cut off from all communication,
inside and outside of the walled capital, were surrounded by an angry and misguided mob that
threatened their lives; nor the joy that thrilled the
world when a single message from the Government
of the United States brought, through our minister,
the first news of the safety of the besieged diplo-
mats.

At the beginning of the nineteenth century there
was not a mile of steam railroad on the globe; now
there are enough miles to make its circuit many
times. Then there was not a line of electric telegraph; now we have a vast mileage traversing all
lands and all seas. God and man have linked the
nations together. No nation can longer be indifferent to any other. And as we are brought more
and more in touch with each other, the less oc-

casion is there for misunderstandings, and the
stronger the disposition, when we have differences
to adjust them in the court of arbitration, which is
the noblest forum for the settlement of international disputes.

My fellow-citizens: Trade statistics indicate
that this country is in a state of unexampled prosperity. The figures are almost appalling. They
show that we are utilizing our fields and forests
and mines, and that we are furnishing profitable
employment to the millions of workingmen throughout the United States, bringing comfort and happiness to their homes, and making it possible to lay
by savings for old age and disability. That all the
people are participating in this great prosperity is
seen in every American community, and shown by
the enormous and unprecedented deposits in our
savings-banks. Our duty is the care and security
of these deposits, and their safe investment demands
the highest integrity and the best business capacity
of those in charge of these depositories of the
people's earnings.

We have a vast and intricate business, built up
through years of toil and struggle, in which every
part of the country has its stake, which will not
permit of either neglect or of undue selfishness.
No narrow, sordid policy will subserve it. The
greatest skill and wisdom on the part of the manu-
facturers and producers will be required to hold
and increase it. Our industrial enterprises, which
have grown to such great proportions, affect the

homes and occupations of the people and the welfare of the country. Our capacity to produce has developed so enormously, and our products have so multiplied, that the problem of more markets requires our urgent and immediate attention. Only a broad and enlightened policy will keep what we have. No other policy will get more. In these times of marvelous business energy and gain we ought to be looking to the future, strengthening the weak places in our industrial and commercial systems, that we may be ready for any storm or strain.

By sensible trade arrangements which will not interrupt our home production, we shall extend the outlets for our increasing surplus. A system which provides a mutual exchange of commodities is manifestly essential to the continued and healthful growth of our export trade. We must not repose in fancied security that we can forever sell everything and buy little or nothing. If such a thing were possible, it would not be best for us or for those with whom we deal. We should take from out customers such of their products as we can use without harm to our industries and labor. Reciprocity is the natural outgrowth of our wonderful industrial development under the domestic policy now firmly established. What we produce beyond our domestic consumption must have a vent abroad. The excess must be relieved through a foreign outlet, and we should sell everywhere we can and buy wherever the buying will enlarge our sales and productions, and thereby make a greater demand for home labor.

The period of exclusiveness is past. The expansion of our trade and commerce is the pressing problem. Commercial wars are unprofitable. A policy of good-will and friendly trade relations will prevent reprisals. Reciprocity treaties are in harmony with the spirit of the times; measures of retaliation are not.

If perchance some of our tariffs are no longer needed for revenue or to encourage and protect our industries at home, why should they not be employed to extend and promote our markets abroad?

Then, too, we have inadequate steamship service. New lines of steamers have already been put in commission between the Pacific Coast ports of the United States and those on the western coasts of Mexico and Central and South America. These should be followed up with direct steamship lines between the eastern coast of the United States and South American ports. One of the needs of the times is direct commercial lines from our vast fields of production to the fields of consumption that we have but barely touched. Next in advantage to having the thing to sell is to have the convenience to carry it to the buyer. We must encourage our merchant marine. We must have more ships. They must be under the American flag, built and manned and owned by Americans. These will not only be profitable in a commercial sense—they will be messengers of peace and amity wherever they go.

We must build the isthmian canal, which will unite the two oceans and give a straight line of water communication with the western coasts of Central and South America and Mexico. The construction of a Pacific cable cannot be longer postponed.

In the furtherance of these objects of national interest and concern you are performing an important part. This exposition would have touched the heart of that American statesman whose mind was ever alert and thought ever constant for a larger commerce and a truer fraternity of the republics of the New World. His broad American spirit is felt and manifested here. He needs no identification to an assemblage of Americans anywhere, for the name of Blaine is inseparably associated with the Pan-American movement which finds its practical and substantial expression, and which we all hope will be firmly advanced, by the Pan-American Congress that assembles this autumn in the capital of Mexico.

The good work will go on. It cannot be stopped. These buildings will disappear, this creation of art and beauty and industry will perish from sight, but their influence will remain to—

"Make it live beyond its too short living,
  With praises and thanksgiving."

Who can tell the new thoughts that have been awakened, the ambitions fired, and the high achievements that will be wrought through this exposition? Let us ever remember that our interest is in concord, not in conflict; and that our real eminence rests in the victories of peace, not those of war. We hope that all who are represented here may be moved to higher and nobler effort for their own and the world's good, and that out of this city may come, not only greater commerce and trade for us all, but, more essential than these, relations of mutual respect, confidence, and friendship which will deepen and endure.

Our earnest prayer is that God will graciously vouchsafe prosperity, happiness, and peace to all neighbors, and like blessings to all the peoples and powers of earth.

Foundations of Progress.

Theodore Roosevelt.

[*The Address from which these extracts are taken was delivered at a public reception at Raleigh, North Carolina, October 19, 1905, and is fairly typical of the hundreds of similar speeches made by this vigorous statesman, who did so much to awaken the virile moral forces of the nation. In this address the President announced his famous doctrine of the "Square Deal."*]

I AM glad here at the capital of North Carolina to have a chance to greet so many of the sons and daughters of your great State. North Carolina's part in our history has ever been high and honorable. It was in North Carolina that the Mecklenburg Declaration of Independence foreshadowed the course taken in a few short months by the representatives of the thirteen colonies assembled in Philadelphia. North Carolina can rightfully say that she pointed us the way which led to the formation of the new Nation. In the Revolution she did many memorable deeds; and the battle of King's Mountain marked the turning point of the Revolutionary War in the South.

But I congratulate you, not only upon your past, but upon your present. I congratulate you upon the great industrial activity shown in your Commonwealth. You are showing in practical fashion your realization of the truth that there must be a foundation of material well-being in order that any community may make real and rapid progress. And

I am happy to say that you are in addition showing in practical fashion your understanding of the great truth that this material well-being, though necessary as a foundation, can only be the foundation, and that upon it must be raised the superstructure of a higher life, if the Commonwealth is to stand as it should stand. More and more you are giving care and attention to education; and education means the promotion not only of industry, but of that good citizenship which rests upon individual rights and upon the recognition by each individual that he has duties as well as rights—in other words, of that good citizenship which rests upon moral integrity and intellectual freedom. The man who fails to be honest and brave both in his political franchise and in his private business contributes to political and social anarchy. Self-government is not an easy thing. Only those communities are fit for it in which the average individual practices the virtues of self-command, of self-restraint, of wise disinterestedness combined with wise self-interest; where the individual possesses common-sense, honesty, and courage.

The position of honor in your parade to-day is held by the Confederate veterans. They by their deeds reflect credit upon their descendants and upon all Americans, both because they did their duty in war and because they did their duty in peace. Now if the young men, their sons, will not only prove that they possess the same power of fealty to an ideal, but will also show the efficiency in the ranks of industrial life that their fathers, the Confederate veterans, showed that they possessed in the ranks of war, the industrial future of this great and typically American Commonwealth is assured.

The extraordinary development of industrialism during the last half century has been due to several causes, but above all to the revolution in the methods of transportation and communication; that is, to steam and to electricity, to the railroad and the telegraph.

When the Government was founded commerce was carried on by essentially the same instruments that had been in use not only among civilized, but among barbarian, nations, ever since history dawned; that is, by wheeled vehicles drawn by animals, by pack trains, and by sailing ships and rowboats. On land this meant that commerce went in slow, cumbrous, and expensive fashion over highways open to all. Normally these highways could not compete with water transportation, if such was feasible between the connecting points.

All this has been changed by the developments of the railroads. Save on the ocean or on lakes so large as to be practically inland seas, transport by water has wholly lost its old position of superiority over transport by land, while, instead of the old highways open to every one on the same terms, but of very limited usefulness, we have new highways—railroads—which are owned by private corporations and which are practically of unlimited, instead of limited, usefulness. The old laws and old customs which were adequate and proper to meet the old conditions need radical readjustment in order to meet these new conditions. The cardinal features in these changed conditions are, first, the fact that the new highway, the railway, is, from the commercial standpoint, of infinitely greater importance in our industrial life than was the old highway, the wagon road; and, second, that this new highway, the railway, is in the hands of private owners, whereas the old highway, the wagon road, was in the hands of the State. The management of the new highway, the railroad, or rather of the intricate web of railroad lines which cover the country, is a task infinitely more difficult, more delicate, and more important than the primitively easy task of acquiring or keeping in order the old highway; so that there is properly no analogy whatever between the two cases.

I do not believe in government ownership of anything which can with propriety be left in private hands, and in particular I should most strenuously object to government ownership of railroads. But I believe with equal firmness that it is out of the question for the Government not to exercise a supervisory and regulatory right over the railroads; for it is vital to the well-being of the public that they should be managed in a spirit of fairness and justice toward all the public. Actual experience has shown that it is not possible to leave the railroads uncontrolled. Such a system, or rather such a lack of system, is fertile in abuses of every kind, and puts a premium upon unscrupulous and ruthless cunning in railroad management; for there are some big shippers and some railroad managers who are always willing to take unfair advantage of their weaker competitors, and they thereby force other big shippers and big railroad men who would like to do decently into similar acts of wrong and injustice, under penalty of being left behind in the race for success. Government supervision is needed quite as much in the interest of the big shipper and of the railroad man who tries to do right as in the interest of the small shipper and the consumer.

Experience has shown that the present laws are defective and need amendment. The effort to prohibit all restraint of competition, whether reasonable or unreasonable, is unwise. What we need is to have some administrative body with ample power to forbid combination that is hurtful to the public, and to prevent favoritism to one individual at the expense of another. In other words, we want an administrative body with the power to secure fair and just treatment as among all shippers who use the railroads—and all shippers have a right to use them. We must not leave the enforcement of such a law merely to the Department of Justice; it is out of the question for the law department of the Government to do what should be purely administrative work. The Department of Justice is to stand behind and co-operate with the administrative body, but the administrative body itself must be given the power to do the work and then held to a strict accountability for the exercise of that power. The delays of the law are proverbial, and what we need is reasonable quickness of action.

If there is in the minds of the Commission any suspicion that a certain railroad is in any shape or way giving rebates or behaving improperly, I wish the Commission to have power as a matter of right, not as a matter of favor, to make a full and exhaustive investigation of the receipts and expenditures of the railroad, so that any violation or evasion of the law may be detected. This is not a revolutionary proposal on my part, for I only wish the same power given in reference to railroads that is now exercised as a matter of course by the national bank examiners as regards national banks. My object in giving these additional powers to the administrative body representing the Government— the Interstate Commerce Commission or whatever it may be—is primarily to secure a real and not a sham control to the Government representatives. The American people abhor a sham, and with this abhorrence I cordially sympathize. Nothing is more injurious from every standpoint than a law which is merely sound and fury, merely pretence, and not capable of working out tangible results. I hope to see all the power that I think it ought to have granted to the Government; but I would far rather see only some of it granted, but really granted, than see a pretence of granting all in some shape that really amounts to nothing.

It must be understood, as a matter of course, that if this power is granted it is to be exercised with wisdom and caution and self-restraint. The Interstate Commerce Commissioner or other Government official who failed to protect a railroad that was in the right against any clamor, no matter how violent, on the part of the public, would be guilty of as gross a wrong as if he corruptly rendered an improper service to the railroad at the expense of the public. When I say a square deal I mean a square deal; exactly as much a square deal for the rich man as for the poor man; but no more. Let each stand on his merits, receive what is due him, and be judged according to his deserts. To more he is not entitled, and less he shall not have.

The Philippines.

WILLIAM H. TAFT.

[*From Address at Carabaos' Banquet, Washington, D. C., January 29, 1910.*]

HE Philippine question or the Philippines as a subject present themselves to me in two different lights —in three perhaps: One in the picturesqueness of the reminiscences that come to you as you look back to the three or four years of life that you spent in that beautiful country under conditions sometimes of privation, sometimes of discomfort; but the discomfort, the privations disappear in your memory; and when the beauties and the strangeness of those islands and the life in them come back to you, and you do feel —I feel it myself—I know it exists, that "Call of the East" that Kipling speaks of in his poem, that makes you yearn to be back again on that beautiful Luneta in Manila, and see the sun go down over the mountains of Marivailes—a picture matchless in all its coloring rises in your memory to make you thank God that you have had the opportunity to be there.

Now in the history of our stay in the Philippines there were times when the army was to the front, when nothing but war was there; when the Filipino, fighting as best he could and taking the instruments that the Lord had given him, among which were stealth and easy change from being a friend to an enemy and back again—there arose between the army and those little people a feeling of enmity, a feeling of contempt on the part of the American soldier for soldiers who would resort to the ruses that they resorted to, and which led to the killing of our brave men. It was inevitable that for a time a bitterness should exist and a contempt arise. Then you came, after the war disappeared, into contact with that people, and found them after all a simple people, a courteous people, a people under the influence of the tropical sun not too energetic, but a people who, childlike in their dependence, if they gave it to you, could win your affections as few people could—at least that is the way I felt.

Then there comes what the army did there. It was upon the army that there fell the burden of eliminating an insurrection that extended the islands' full length, and they had to be divided up into five hundred different posts and they had to put small detachments of the army under command of lieutenants and second lieutenants, and even sergeants, and trust to the ability of the non-commissioned officers and the young-commissioned officers to carry on independent campaigns in the neighborhood of the post to which they were assigned, in stamping out this insurrection. No army, and I assert it without any fear of contradiction, could have offered that knowledge, that independence of judgment, that self-reliance on the part of those young officers that enabled it as a whole ultimately and quietly and softly—and—I had almost said—peaceably to bring about a condition of pacification in the islands and to stamp out an insurrection so difficult to overcome. And in those campaigns there was an opportunity for individual bravery and courage that is not exceeded by any opportunity in the Civil War or any other war that this country was engaged in.

And this Signal Corps which was referred to to-night in a jocular way, may point to a record of loss in death and wounds in those islands that I think has been equaled by no other signal corps, and perhaps by no other corps in any other army.

What we went to the Philippines to do was to defeat the fleet of an enemy in a war that was begun as no other war in the history of the world— no other foreign war—from pure altruism; and we got into the islands and we had them on our hands before we knew what the consequences were to be. And when they came into our hands there seemed to us—at least to those of us who were responsible —the obligation of doing the right thing. The question was, "What are we going to do?" Are we going to let those islands go into chaos; are we going to turn them back to Spain with the charges against the domination of Spain that were made? Or are we to take them ourselves and develop them as best we may under our institutions? President McKinley went into those islands with great reluctance and assumed the burdens which were most heavy to him of introducing a government there which should be the best for the islands. Now, of course it is a matter of dispute how good a government we have there. Having taken part in its formation, perhaps it is improper—or at least I speak as a prejudiced witness—but I believe that the ten years of government in the Philippines has made that people a far happier people than they would have been under any other conditions that might have been presented by our taking a different course. They enjoy to-day a free trade tariff on the one hand and the right to sell in a protected market on the other. That was long coming, but we have ultimately secured it. We have saved the rice of our friend the Senator from South Carolina. We were asked to stave off a little bit of the injury to the tobacco and the sugar of other parts of the country. They are now beginning, as I believe an industrial progress there that means an elevation of those people intellectually and spiritually in such a way that we can continue to extend to them, from time to time, additional self-government. We now have put them under one chamber which is elected popularly, sharing the government with a commission upon which there are a number of Filipinos.

A third question which arises is the effect of the Spanish War and our going to the Philippines upon the country at large, upon our standing before the nations of the world, and upon our opportunities for usefulness as a prosperous, powerful country. And I think in that record perhaps the Spanish War and what followed are more important than in any other aspect. I know it is easy to make fun of a proposition that we as a nation have an obligation because of our power and wealth to assist other nations that may be thrown upon us in such a way as to call for our aid and support; but I do believe in the brotherhood of nations, and I do believe that nations are like members of a community and a neighborhood where the wealthy and the powerful and the more fortunate owe it to the weaker and the less fortunate to assist them when circumstances point in that direction.

As a matter of fact the result of the Philippine War, our ownership of the Philippines, our ownership of Porto Rico, our friendship for and close relation to Cuba, our assertion of an interest in South America and an interest in the Isthmus bringing us into close relations with Central America, and our assertion of a right to the "open door" in China, have put us in a position forefront among the nations of the world; and I believe we have no right to neglect the opportunity to take such a position or the opportunity to use that position for the progress of civilization in the world. Now the result of that war, short as it was, involving as little blood as it did, was remarkable. The expansion of the United States as a great world power dates from that time. We are not going about seeking to aggrandize ourselves, seeking for territory in China or anywhere else.

We are building the Panama Canal now for the benefit of the world, and at the same time to aid us in our commerce and to strengthen and double the force of our Navy. The broadening of our people with regard to those problems, the liberalizing of the army, or making the army a body—and especially the officers—a body of well-read gentlemen, men of affairs—all date from that time.

It may be as I say that I am a prejudiced witness. I am. Nevertheless a witness may be prejudiced, but he may have such an advantage in opportunities for observation which are denied to those who are only free from prejudice, as to make his evidence better than the judge who sits on the case. I am sorry I did not have the opportunity of welcoming to the Philippine Islands my Brother Tillman. There were some of his Democratic brethren whom I entertained there with great pleasure and into their sphere of vision I think we introduced some things that changed their aspect, changed their views I should say, of the situation there. They deplored what we had to do, but they thought we were doing it well. The truth is, while my friend the Senator comes from South Carolina and the South, I think I know something of the attitude of his brethren in the South with reference to the Philippine Islands and this general policy of expansion, and I think we could have a vote on

that alone without introducing the race question
and all that sort of thing—the wisdom of our taking the Philippines as we have taken them, and developing them as we are developing them, teaching
them English and extending to them, as they show
themselves fit, self-government.   Then the time
may come, and I hope it may come soon, when
they shall be ready to take over a government like
that of Australia or Canada, and I say so, not because we might not be willing to part with them,
but because they will find that under the present
arrangement, under the tariff as arranged there and
the tariff as arranged here, it is greatly to their
advantage to retain some sort of bond, no matter
how light, which will justify their continuing to
enjoy the benefit of our markets with a free trade
tariff toward the Orient.

There were times in the Philippines when the
nervous strain upon those who were responsible
was tremendous and the more tremendous because
we were so far removed, it seemed, from Washington and the people of the United States.   There
were times, and they were many, when the beauties
of life in that country, when the associations that
we made there, when the feeling that we did have
a people who were grateful at times and who listened to us as children, depending on us and having
confidence in us—gave us a pleasure in doing the
good which we thought we were doing, a pleasure
that knows no measure, for there is nothing in life
equal to the consciousness of having attempted to

do good for a people and having in a measure succeeded.

There is one other thought that I wanted to give you, and that was in relation to the carabao. There is no animal that is the friend of the Filipino like the carabao. He moves slowly, he moves deliberately, but he moves always in the right direction, and he gets there after a time without respect to obstacles. It is unwise, in dealing with the Filipino or in dealing with anything in the tropics, to suppose that you are going to make headway suddenly. The carabao represents the right policy in working out the problems in the East, and I congratulate you on having selected that animal as an indication that you know how to accomplish things in the Philippines. Ill as I was in 1902, for three or four months, and confined to my bed in the First Reserve Hospital in the Philippines, Mrs. Moses sent me a full set of volumes, and in one of the chapters entitled Kipling's "Naulahka," I found a verse that gave me a great deal of consolation, and if I can remember it I want to recite it as a justification for your selection of this animal as typical of your policy and our policy and our hopes and yours in the Philippines:

"Now it is not good for the Christian's health to hustle the Aryan brown;
For the Christian riles and the Aryan smiles and he weareth the Christian down;
And the end of the fight is a tombstone white, with the name of the late deceased;
And the epitaph drear, "A fool lies here, who tried to hustle the East."